BEYOND THE BLACK MOUNTAIN

First published in 1990
Reprinted October 1990
by Quest Books
2 Slievenabrock Avenue, Newcastle, Co. Down, N. Ireland BT33 OHZ.

Typeset by Textflow Services Limited, Belfast.
Printed in Northern Ireland by
The Universities Press (Belfast) Limited.

British Library Cataloguing-in-Publication Data
Slader, Bert
Beyond The Black Mountain: a journey around
the Ulster of yesterday.
1. Northern Ireland. Social Life, 1920-1949 - Bibliographies
1. Title
941. 60822092

ISBN 1-872027-01-6

Illustrated by Wilfrid Capper
The illustrations show Northern Ireland as it was in 1939-1946 and include
original sketches made by Wilfrid during that period.

BEYOND THE BLACK MOUNTAIN

BERT SLADER

A journey around the Ulster of yesterday

Illustrated by Wilfrid Capper

QUEST BOOKS

The Road to the Quay Ballycastle

Contents

To those who helped me on the way

Walter, Harry and Jim were my companions in the Bog Meadows, along the River Lagan and on the Black Mountain. I salute them across the years. Stanley was there too and he also had the patience and fortitude to bear with me on the cycle journey. All four shared their teenage years with me and, although we then went our separate ways, I remember their friendship with a profound feeling of gratitude.

Although our journey around the Province was so long ago, I still feel a sense of obligation to everyone who helped Stanley and me on our way. I owe it also to those who befriended or helped me as I was beginning to discover Northern Ireland over those years as an evacuee or during our Boys' Brigade camps.

No one I know, knows the countryside and the by-ways of this Province better than Wilfrid Capper. It is to him and his friends in organisations like the Ulster Society for the Preservation of the Countryside, that we all owe our gratitude for their work over the past 60 years, in preserving the best of Northern Ireland's countryside to this day.

It is my great delight that Wilfrid has illustrated 'Beyond the Black Mountain' and I acknowledge my special thanks to him for agreeing to do so and for helping me develop my own appreciation of our country's outdoors over the years.

In the mountains and as a Sports Council colleague, Dick Jones has shared a great deal more with me than designing a book but my thanks are due to him for his help in the final stages of the presentation of this volume.

I am glad to acknowledge the help of all those friends who gave me support and practical assistance. In particular, I remember those who have encouraged me through their letters and comments and who have become new friends since the publication of my first book, Pilgrims' Footsteps.

Come with me, new friend or old, on a journey around the Ulster of yesterday.

Bert Slader
2 Slievenabrock Avenue
Newcastle Co. Down BT33 0HZ

vi

For

THOMAS

CHAPTER 1

The Yellow Convoy

There were advantages in growing up in Belfast in the nineteen thirties and early forties, although, it has to be said, that this might not have been immediately obvious to a stranger. It was, of course, an industrial city, split by sectarian loyalties and for six of those years there was a war on. But it was a friendly town with something to interest a young boy around every corner. There were red trams on the Donegall Road, horse-drawn delivery vehicles in the street and a proper railway line used by magnificent steam engines, which cut through the city near where I lived. In July and August there were huge parades in Sandy Row and the Falls Road, with drums, banners and bands and no vagueness about the tribal allegiance of each locality.

But for me the real advantage was that the green fields met the city streets and the countryside was never more than a short walk away.

In one direction the River Lagan meandered through County Down, flanked by great wooded estates, whose fences were no defence against young boys. Along the river and its canal was a path by which huge horses towed barges laden with raw materials and finished goods to and from the factories of Ulster.

In another direction were the hills of Antrim, their southern limits forming a ridge which closed in the north side of the Lagan valley. The best-known summit was Cave Hill but it was at the other end of the ridge, looking down on the harbour and Belfast Lough.

Above our part of the city was the Black Mountain and we supposed it was so called because the low clouds often darkened its green slopes. We knew that the way to it, from where we lived on the Donegall Road, was up the hill to the end of that road, across the Falls Road and along the Whiterock Road to the base of the mountains.

A few years later this was a route which would become familiar to many of Belfast's citizens who were not especially interested in walking, nor would all of them have expected to be travelling through this part of the city by choice.

A short distance from the ridge which led to the top of the Black Mountain, where the farmland gave way to the open hill-side, was the Hatchet Field. It was really two huge fields, one representing the shaft of the hatchet, the other the blade. We had heard that there was a path along the underside of the handle and that this was the route to the summit.

On a good day it was possible to see the way quite clearly from our home streets. Simple names they might be, the Hatchet Field, and the Black Mountain but, for us, there was a strange, exciting lure in being able to see these places without having reached them.

The war came stealthily but all-pervasively to Belfast in 1939 with identity cards, gas masks in cardboard boxes, food rationing, air-raid drill and plans for the evacuation of children and adults not involved in the war effort.

As in the rest of the United Kingdom, the adults of Northern

Ireland braced themselves for a long and bitter struggle. Children, even those as young as I was, knew that something terrible had happened and worse was to come. Serious grown-up conversations and the gloomy voices of announcers on the wireless created an atmosphere of strain and dread of what the future might hold. But for me the strongest memory is of excitement at the prospect of the imminent battles. I was just turned nine years old, old enough to understand that this was a momentous and dangerous time but young enough never to have experienced real fear.

Early in the war a spokesman for the German Third Reich predicted a blitzkrieg programme of air raids on the United Kingdom which would bring 'a chaos of fire explosions and buildings collapsing'. The first air-raid alerts sounded in Belfast less than a month later but they were false alarms. There was a feeling that Northern Ireland would not be bombed because the Germans did not want to jeopardise the neutrality of Eire. It was a conviction not shared by many Protestants.

In July 1940 I was evacuated to a farm in North Antrim, just before my tenth birthday. Two of us were destined for the same billet. The son of my school's principal teacher was meant to go with me but he, like most of the others who were supposed to be evacuated on that day, stayed at home.

I arrived at Ballymoney Railway Station with a crowd of other evacuees but knowing no one. A woman from the reception committee checked me in and expressed surprise that I was on my own. I was given a lift to my billet by a farmer and had to share the back seat of his little car with a sheep. Petrol was scarce, he told me and there was no point making two journeys half empty when a full one would do.

This was the first time I had been in such close contact with a farm animal and the smell remains in my memory, slightly acrid, damp, not altogether unpleasant, but strong; a most powerful, all-pervading smell. The sheep took advantage of this close acquaintance and did her droppings on my shoe. I shook them off, nudged her over a bit with my knee and was too embarrassed to say anything.

The farm was near Moss-side and beside a landmark known as the Dry Arch, a bridge which carried one road over another road rather than a river. It was called locally 'the drey erch' and it was some time before I was able to translate and thus realise the significance of the name.

The Hodges family treated me like a son of the house. Mr Hodges was a hard-working North Antrim farmer who expected his family and his evacuee to help when necessary. His wife was a cheerful, motherly woman who always seemed to be busy but had time to help a ten-year-old boy to adjust to living away from home for the first time. The eldest son was at University. The eldest daughter was old enough to be a grown-up and was kind and patient with me. The younger son was called Billy. He was a year or so older than I and we became firm friends. The family was completed by a baby girl, Alice, and, at this distance in time, I can remember her as a happy contented child, who only cried when she was hungry.

I learned to milk a cow, to tread flax in a dam, to catch eels, to drive cattle, to stack turf, to find the eggs the hens and ducks laid and to bud potatoes. Although some of the farm work was hard for a city ten-year-old it was a wonderful time.

The only hated chore was budding the potatoes. We did this job inside a shed on a wet day, rubbing the buds off potatoes which had been stored over the winter in mounds called clamps. In the clamp they had been covered with straw and soil to protect them from the frost. When they were dug out they were damp, sticky, sprouting white shoots through a coating of mud. We had to deal with a great pile of them on the floor of an outhouse. The buds were removed to keep the potatoes from becoming uneatable and to do that we had to scrape the soil off with our fingers and nick each shoot out at its base with a thumb nail.

It was not the dirt of the job. Young boys are rarely adverse to working in wet soil and mud. The potatoes were crawling with insects, beetles, centipedes, bugs of every description. They crawled all over us, on our clothes, in our hair, up our arms and legs. Mr Hodges had his trousers bottoms tucked into his socks but Billy and I were wearing shorts and had no such protection. It was the only time I can ever remember fervently wishing I was old enough to wear long trousers.

Billy and I roamed the countryside when not required to work, wandering through the bogs and bushes and copses of trees, exploring, hiding, fighting an invisible enemy across the fields and open country.

In the autumn I came back home, to strict rationing, shortages, soldiers in the street, the black-out, air-raid sirens, the war news on the wireless and the spectacular sight of immense barrage balloons floating above the city.

Belfast had its first air-raid at the beginning of April 1941. My place of shelter was under the kitchen table. There I listened to the drone of the bombers, and the sharp crack of anti-aircraft guns. Some of the bombs whined and whistled as they fell before exploding with a great crumping roar as they hit the ground.

The trekking, as it was called, started next evening. From our front door we could see a stream of people, like a crowd on the way to a football match at Celtic Park. They carried bags of food and blankets and were walking out of town on the Donegall Road, heading for the slopes of the Black Mountain to escape the destruction of the bombers. For many families it became a daily ritual. Each evening they left home in their thousands after an early tea and came back to the city next morning to go to work.

At first they were called 'The Yellow Convoy' but I can remember my mother saying that no one was prepared to use this insult after the Easter Raids a few days later.

On Easter Tuesday night about 200 enemy bombers attacked the city of Belfast for 5 hours. Our house shook and rattled. From my shelter under the table it seemed as if the whole enemy force was overhead and their bombs were exploding all around us. But, although we were now involved in the battle, I can still remember feeling much more excitement than fear. Our only damage was a picture shaken off the wall.

Next day the city seemed devastated. It was one of the heaviest raids on any British city except London during the war. The destruction was on a colossal scale. Thousands of houses were demolished or damaged, parts of the city were obliterated, over 700 people were killed. Many were buried in mass graves in the city's cemeteries. Even in death they were separated by religion, those who were Catholics being identified by their rosary beads or holy medals.

If the first official evacuation had been a failure the previous year because so few people were prepared to leave home, there was no reluctance now. Immediately after the Easter raid 100,000 people left the city. I was evacuated again, to a cousin's home at Waringstown in County Down. This time I had Jackie, the son of a neighbour in Belfast, two young nieces, Elaine and Dorothy, and Charles, an even younger nephew, for company.

I learned how to make butter, to find eggs when the hens laid them away from the hen-house and to play cricket with proper bats and pads and stumps with bails. Waringstown was a village famous for its cricket.

There were so many of us as evacuees it caused consternation at the local school. We had to stand in class at first because the teacher did not want us to share desks with the village pupils. If there was any unexplained mischief we were blamed.

On one hilarious occasion, when the Principal was caning a miscreant on the hand, the cane broke cleanly in two on the first slap. Careful examination showed that the cane had been sawn through half-way and the teacher stared at the two pieces, unable to believe the evidence before his eyes. He looked up and seeing the astonishment on his face at the utter effrontery of this act of sabotage, we roared with laughter.

We were all kept in that afternoon, which was reckoned by us, to be a much more unpleasant punishment than caning. Although I had no idea of the identity of the culprit, like everyone else in the class, I shared his triumph. The detention dragged on interminably but it was worth every minute of it. There was nothing the Principal could have done to us which would have taken away the feeling that, on the day, we had won the battle.

At my cousin's small holding one of our favourite jobs was taking the cow back to its field after milking. One day there was a bull in a neighbouring field and he smashed his way through the fence to chase us, or rather more likely, to chase the cow. I pushed Elaine, Dorothy and Charles into a hole in a thick hedge and we hid in its depths. The bull roared and stamped. He crashed past us but the young cow could run and made her escape down the lane. We stayed in the hedge until the danger was past and, at the time, I was amazed how bravely the three young children reacted. It was only later I realised that it was probably due in part to the confidence they had in me as someone much older, me being eleven at the time.

Warringstown Parish Church

One night we were allowed out very late to see a great glow in the sky. Belfast was 20 miles away but it seemed as if the whole city must be on fire. For the first time in the war I felt fear. I knew that my father would be on fire-watching duty on the roof of a linen factory. My mother was a maternity nurse attending mothers who gave birth at home, as most women did then. I knew too that babies never seemed to choose the most convenient time to be born and that my mother could well have been called out during the raid.

This must have been the last big raid on the city on the night of the 4th May 1941. It was a 3 hour fire blitz, again delivered by about 200 enemy bombers using oil bombs, high explosive bombs, parachute mines, delayed action bombs and incendiaries by the hundred. Although much more material damage was inflicted than during the Easter Tuesday raid far fewer people were killed because so many had been evacuated from the city or had trekked out on to the mountain to shelter for the night.

Later, when I came back home, I heard the scene described by those who had trekked to the Black Mountain. They were perched on the hill-side above an enormous blaze as if the whole city was being burned in a gigantic bonfire. The flames lit up the sky. Clouds of black smoke billowed upwards. Then a huge mine or an oil dump would explode and shoot a mass of sparks and flames above the conflagration. It was a sight they would never forget and which was remembered, and often talked about later in the war, when German cities were being subjected to similar treatment by Allied aircraft.

Next day, in my safe haven at Waringstown, I said nothing, but each morning I watched anxiously for the postman. Four days later the letter came. It had been a bad raid, my mother said, but they were both all right and my father had the tail fin of an incendiary bomb for me when I came home.

There were no more raids after the month of May and I came home again at the end of the summer to go to Grosvenor Senior Public Elementary School. I had enjoyed the country but it was good to be back home in Belfast.

The school was over a mile away by the streets but there was a short-cut. It meant scaling a huge stone wall which had once enclosed the grounds of an asylum. It was called locally the Slim Wall. 'Slim', I suppose, being an abbreviation for asylum, and climbing it was one of the supreme challenges for boys who lived in the district.

Someone, worried about the danger of a serious fall, must have complained to Mr McMaster, the school's Principal, and he called on the culprits to own up. Three of us did so and appeared before him in his study. To our amazement we were congratulated for our honesty instead of being caned. It was all the more surprising as our Principal was famous as a caning man and so good at it that boys hardened the palms of their hands on the edge of window-sills to be ready for him. However, perhaps he felt that the ascent of the wall was an understandable challenge. He let us off with a warning and a wicked grin as he told us what would happen should we try it again.

The American troops came to Northern Ireland at the beginning of 1942, so many of them that they seemed to have invaded Belfast. They chewed gum incessantly, even it seemed, when eating, drinking milk from pint bottles or smoking, They were friendly, self-confident, generous and very obviously bored because there was so little to do on their time off.

Their uniforms were made of a fine, smooth material very different from the rough battle dress of the British soldiers. Accustomed as we were to strict rationing, many of them looked over-fed and un-fit. Our elders seriously doubted their potential as fighting soldiers.

They drove around in jeeps and moved and talked in a relaxed, casual way which I had only seen in American films. To me, their most surprising habit was the way some of them walked. It was a long, slow, loose-limbed saunter with a hip-rolling action as if they were cowboys who had just ridden into town and were mooseying along the board walk to the saloon. It was from a different world than the Belfast dander.

Horses were a common sight in the city, many coal, milk and bread carts were still horse-drawn. Shortage of fuel was only one of the reasons, it was still cheaper to run a horse that a van. It may have been picturesque but it also meant that there was horse dung on the streets and a great many flies about.

Once the Americans had been established for a while, many of the Belfast flies disappeared. It was a mystery to our parents until we told them that American soldiers were spraying oil over the Bog Meadows. Obviously the oil had destroyed the breeding grounds of many of the flies but it also ruined the meadow as our playground.

The Bog Meadows started at the top of our street. It was a huge area of open country with little streams and a river, with humps and hollows and boggy patches which we knew how to avoid and which froze over in winter. As twelve-year-olds it was our favourite place for playing and, at this stage of the war, it was as far as we were allowed to roam. For months it remained an oily mess until nature intervened and the rain flushed the black scum away. My friends and I were annoyed with these strangers who had ruined our meadow playground for so long and all to kill a few flies.

The American soldiers went so far down in my estimation because of this incident that it was not until the latter stages of the war and they had proved themselves in battle, that I was able to accept them as friends and allies again.

Shaw's Bridge

CHAPTER 2

Roast Potatoes and Red-Hot Lingoes

Once our parents were sure that the air-raids had ceased, we were allowed to venture further from home. Without thinking about the reason we always went away from the mountain and towards the River Lagan. The year I was thirteen, three of us began the summer holidays by walking, almost every afternoon, the four miles to Shaw's Bridge on the outskirts of the city and to the towpath beyond.

Walter, Harry and I brought raw potatoes in our pockets and a box of matches. We explored the river and the woods, climbed trees, searched for nuts and collected dry wood for a fire. Below us, the barges glided past, towed by great, powerful horses and steered by calm, pipe-smoking men.

In a secret place we lit a fire with dry grass and twigs for kindling and dead wood for fuel. The fire would smoke and splutter and then blaze away. In its embers we placed the potatoes and found it very hard to wait until they were properly roasted before we poked one out of the ashes to see if it was ready to eat. It felt as if we were living rough, like soldiers or nomads or tramps, surviving in wild country, learning the tricks of the trade, like cooking on a wood fire.

In the books about real North American Indians, not the Cowboys and Indians variety, I had read that the Indians took care of the wild forests and regarded the trees as their friends. So we were careful not to damage the living trees and to make sure the fire was out before we left, but we felt that the fallen wood was ours for the taking. We never considered that we might be trespassing and no one ever came to challenge us or chase us away. Very occasionally we would see someone walking on the towpath and when we were seen by a lighterman, riding his great silent craft down river, he would wave as if he was glad to see us.

11

The Lagan Canal was built in the 18th century to link Belfast with Lough Neagh. Using the lough, boats were able to connect with the Newry Canal and thus to Portadown, Newry and the sea at Carlingford Lough.

The Lagan Canal used sections of the river and this meant that, for part of the outward journey from Belfast, the barges had to be towed upstream against the flow. There were also the problems of coping with low water in summer and flooding in winter. The stretch between Belfast and Lisburn, the banks of which we over-looked, was opened in 1763 and it proved to be the most used section.

In Ulster the barges were called lighters and the haulers, the men who looked after the towing horses, were known as horse drivers. A lighterman's family might well have travelled with him on the boat but it was the horses and the horse drivers who did the hard physical work.

At the time we were visiting the river, which was during the war, the Canal Company was subsidised by the Government to encourage the saving of fuel. The water-way was never as success-ful as had been hoped but it continued to be used through the nineteen forties and into the fifties. The last lighter load to Lisburn was hauled in 1954 and, when the M1 motorway was built, the canal was destroyed beyond all hope of reinstatement.

When one of us spotted a lighter in the distance, it was our great delight to find a vantage point and watch the big barge glide by. Going upstream, the horse driver would be on the tow path urging his great animal on with shouts of encouragement and the jingling of the horse harness.

One day, on the way home, we took a short-cut across a bend of the river's meandering. As we crossed a field above the trees we were chased by a bull and ran for the steep bank which led down to the river. The advice in a book from our local library flashed across my mind ...

'chased by a bear – run down the slope.
chased by a bull – run across the slope.'

... or was it the other way about?
There was no time to dither.
'Across the slope!' I yelled and ran. The others followed me

Third Lock — Lagan Canal

diagonally down towards the towpath fence and we jumped it like high-class cross-country runners. The bull stood at the top of the slope, legs splayed, stamping and snorting.

'How did you know which way to run?' Said one of my friends in a tone of admiration he had never used to me before.

'I read it in a book about travelling in the back-woods in America.' I said with as much modesty as I could manage but anxious not to disclose, that even though the ploy had worked, I was still not sure that I had remembered it the right way around.

As we trudged the four miles back home I was closely questioned about this book on the back-woods as if I had been keeping it a secret. I had to promise that I would show them the shelf at the Donegall Road Library with the books on walking, tramping, living in the open air.

Our parents need not have worried that we were wandering so far from home each day. The real danger was much nearer at hand.

Our street stretched away from the Donegall Road past a factory and alongside the great wedge of open country of the Bog Meadows which was the no-man's-land on either side of the border between Catholic and Protestant Belfast. The actual frontier was a small dirty stream called the Blackstaff although I am not sure we were aware then that it had a proper name. To us it was the Blackie and that seemed appropriate enough because it accurately described the colour of its water. It flowed from the meadows under a bridge on the Donegall Road which was accepted as the precise division between the Unionist and Republican quarters in the west of the city.

On one side of the invisible line were larger than life-size, gable-wall paintings of King William astride a prancing white charger. His Highness was dressed in a red jacket, white breeches and a bright blue cocked hat to ensure we knew whose side he was fighting for. The legend announced that he was ...

'Of Noble, Pious and Immortal Memory'

and in ʾven larger script we were instructed to...

'Remember 1690'

Across the Blackie, between us and the Black Mountain, there was a gable wall which looked the whole of Unionist West Belfast straight in the eye. On it, in huge yellow letters it said ...

'SILENCE IS GOLDEN IRA'

in case anyone might need reminding that when they crossed the line they were entering Republican territory.

Were those who painted the words aware that they were quoting the second part of an ancient Swiss inscription? ...

'Speech is silvern, Silence is golden'

or that Thomas Carlyle, who first brought it into prominence in the English language, felt he would rather have expressed it ...

'Speech is of Time, Silence is of Eternity'.

Communication is never guaranteed when people share a common language. Argument produces winners and losers and promotes conflict, not justice and harmony. In this country, will we ever learn to listen with consideration of each other's point of view? Will we ever speak with understanding of each other's aspirations?

In the early nineteen forties there was no lull in the sectarian conflict because of the war. Sensing a German victory, the Irish Republican Army became more active in the United Kingdom. Conscription was not applied in Northern Ireland and in spite of the fact that many Catholics as well as Protestants were volunteering for the Armed Forces, there was doubt amongst Protestants about the loyalty and commitment of Catholics to the Allied cause. There were rumours of bonfires and much rejoicing in nationalist parts of the city when there was news of an Allied set-back – like the retreat from Dunkirk or the sinking of a Royal Navy ship. The Post Office on the Donegall Road had an armed guard because of the threat of an IRA raid.

Government posters carried the message that....

'Careless Talk Costs Lives'.

Although it was hard to imagine a German spy in Belfast, loyalists believed that spies operated without hindrance across the border. There was resentment too, not only because Eire had chosen to remain neutral but because the Free State apparently continued to maintain friendly links with Germany and Italy. It was well-known that many individual Irishmen from the South had joined the British Army to fight on the Allied side but as a country, Ireland was regarded as being against the Allies, on the premise that 'those who are not for us are against us'.

Great bitterness was caused by the fact that the South of Ireland depended on the Allied convoys for food and trade but refused to allow the warships which protected the convoys against the U-Boats to use the ports in the west of Ireland.

A wind of distrust was being sown which another generation of Catholics would reap as a whirlwind of antagonism as they tried to discover a fairer place in Ulster society.

My parents actively discouraged me from believing the worst of these stories during the war years. Soon after the war ended, I made my first visit to Dublin at the age of fifteen to play rugby for my school. We were received with great kindness and treated to enormous meals by our opponents. At dinner in the school after the game, a priest carved an immense roast with a carving knife as big as a fighting sword. It was like a scene from a medieval banquet. The game itself was an exciting match and next day I featured in an action picture in one of the principal daily papers.

However, in a city street, I was amazed and affronted to come upon a business called the Swastika Laundry, which may indeed still be in business. At the time I was not aware that the swastika had its origins in Eastern religion, only that it was the emblem of the Third Reich. Our local laundry was, and probably not by accident, called the Monarch. However, seeing the hated symbol of the Nazis displayed so blatantly in Dublin I felt I was in a foreign country which had played no part in defeating Hitler. Although this incident did not spoil the trip, it had a most disorientating effect. In spite of the border, I had always thought of Ireland as one country. But how could this be if the whole country had not been on the same side during the war? It took three more years of rugby trips, to play school and inter-provincial games to help resolve this dilemma of identity.

Many years later I saw the swastika painted on a Buddhist stupa shrine in the Himalayas and thought of the laundry in Dublin as well as the Third Reich. And even though I knew that in this setting the swastika was a symbol of good, of well-being, I still found it profoundly distasteful.

But in 1943, it was in the Bog Meadows that the other war, the holy war, fought by teenage boys, was waged. As if it was not enough to be fighting Hitler the lads of Belfast had to do battle amongst themselves.

My friends and I knew that the holy war had already started, probably because the preparations for the celebrations of the twelfth of July had begun, but we were too busy with our trips to the River Lagan to go to see it for three or four days.

Then one morning after breakfast we walked up the street and turned the factory corner to satisfy our curiosity. The battle lines were clearly drawn and the hostilities had begun. On either side of the Blackie were hordes of young boys flinging projectiles and abuse at each other across the dirty stream. Each side was far enough back from the stream to be out of range of all but the very best of the throwers but well inside shouting distance.

The Protestants were 'prods'. The Catholics were 'taigs'. The chants and insults were offensive, blasphemous, profane, sectarian. They featured the Pope, the King, Cromwell, the Black and Tans, the Irish Martyrs, the RUC, 1690 and the Battle of the Boyne.

We stood against the factory wall and watched in awe. We were fascinated and took care to stand well back in case we might be drawn into the combat. Small street skirmishes were fairly common but this was in a different dimension entirely. It was warfare on a grand scale. There were so many warriors on either side, it seemed as if most of the boys of the entire district had been conscripted.

On the nationalist side, workmen had left a large pile of sharp stones for road mending. This was a ready-made arsenal and well out of the reach of raiders. The loyalist boys had brought their own ammunition. Each carried a supply of stones in the front of his jersey, holding the tail of it out with one hand.

One of the waste products of the factory was a thin, stiff, steel rod about fifteen inches long called a lingo. These were now proving useful as missiles. Lingoes were easy to throw and made an ominous whirring sound as they flew through the air. Small fires had been lit to heat the lingoes so that they could be plucked from the fire using a glove or a rag and hurled red-hot at the enemy.

While we watched, and in spite of the force of the bombardment on either side, we saw no sign of any casualties. Providence, discretion and the Blackie were playing their parts well.

On the Protestant side, a small band of boys assembled and began to march up and down waving sticks and Union Jacks and singing Orange songs. The words of Dolly's Brae and The Sash My Father Wore rang out as if they were practising for the Twelfth. In opposition the Catholic boys on the other bank roared out the Soldier's Song and The Wearing Of The Green.

A few optimistic stone-throwers advanced towards the Blackie and tried to land a missile in the midst of the opposition's marching throng, hoping for a lucky strike like that of King Harold at the Battle of Hastings. The bands of marchers were too big to miss, had they been a little nearer, but the leaders had judged their distance well and the range was tantalizingly just beyond the strength of the best of the throwers.

Suddenly one of the boys with a Union Jack broke away from his band with a wild yell and began to run towards the river shaking his flag, like a lone knight charging the enemy host. He was hit by a stone which almost knocked him over but he pressed on shouting louder. His companions stopped for a moment, caught unawares and watched him charge. There was only one honourable course open to them and they took it, surging after their standard-bearer, yelling and roaring. Now the standard bearer had reached the river and was wading across. The others would have to follow. To keep their courage up they cheered and shook their sticks. To their amazement the enemy turned and ran, not backing away slowly but retreating in full flight.

As the Protestant boys entered the water to follow their knight there was a shout above the clamour of the battle. It was only one word but it stopped them in their tracks. It was clear now that it was not their courageous attack which had made the enemy run.

'POLIS!' the voice roared. Then others took it up,
'Its the Polis! Its a Polis raid!'

From our vantage point against the factory wall we saw the Black Maria skid to a stop on the republican side of the Blackie. Upwards of a dozen young policemen jumped out and gave chase. As we were watching, a second Black Maria roared up our street and stopped with a squeal of brakes at the end of the factory wall.

Forgetting that it was not our war, that we were not involved, or maybe doubting that we would be believed, my friends and I made our escape as the doors of the police van were opened. Neutrality is a luxury not available to all.

We ran at full tilt heading for the depths of the bog. In a few seconds we had reached and passed the loyalist lines. Its members were still gleefully watching their republican foes being chased up the other side of the river and not expecting to be attacked from behind. They looked back, saw policemen running towards them and took off like the greyhounds at Celtic Park Race Track.

As the great horde of us fled across the Bog Meadows it was of some comfort to be able to run fairly quickly and to have so many boys between me and the police. Innocent bystanders we may have been a few minutes earlier but not now. We were guilty by association.

It proved useful to be so familiar with the bog, to be aware of the marshy patches where it was possible to sink thigh deep and to know the best crossing places over its streams.

Our route across the heart of the meadows was called The Jumps. We knew it well. It led directly over the bog on the best ground, leading from stream to stream, crossing each one at a suitable place for jumping. Usually we had trouble clearing a few of the bigger jumps, sometimes the nerve would fail and we would not even try, but not to-day. We fairly flew over The Jumps and the further we went the further we seemed to be ahead of the pack.

However, that seemed no reason to slow down and we kept going as hard as we could until we reached a row of houses along a road called Stockman's Lane. There was no other way to reach the roadway so we climbed the back fence of one of the gardens, slipped quietly past the side of the house and let ourselves out through the front gate.

It took us over a hour to walk back home by the roads and it was well after dinner time at one o'clock when I arrived. It would have been hard to explain to my mother why we had run from the police when we were not involved so I said nothing about the Bog Meadows War. Eventually she asked me where I had been. It was said in a conversational tone, asked merely out of interest.

'Out.' I said cheerily, being accustomed to using the teenager's technique of giving nothing away, even when there is nothing to hide. She assumed that I had been off on one of my long walks and let the subject drop.

My friends and I had a feeling that the police might be quite active around the district for a while and that they might be asking questions. If challenged, we would have had to admit to having been there on the day of the police raid. It would have been even more difficult to explain to the Royal Ulster Constabulary, than to our parents, why we had fled.

However, fortune favoured the innocent for once and we had the chance to get away for a week. Our Boys' Brigade Company's annual summer camps had been suspended at the beginning of the war but in the summer of 1943, in spite of rationing, shortages of equipment and travel difficulties, the officers had decided that it was time to reinstate this tradition.

CHAPTER 3

Bell Tents and Palliases

Three impatient memories tug at the sleeve of my schoolboy's navy jersey ... the electric shock which flung me on my back when I accidentally touched the side of a Nissen Hut with my elbow ... finding the Cloghmore Stone perched on the hill-side above the sea ... and the night we frightened sleep away by talking bravely about ghosts, as we lay in our tent and listened to a tree creaking and groaning in the wind.

It was my first time at Boys' Brigade Summer Camp, my first experience under canvas. Our bell-tents were pitched in a recently-vacated army camp. It was a rambling, wooded area, walled in, probably once part of a grand estate. We had explored the site, looking for souvenirs of war, but the soldiers had left nothing of real value to us, no used cartridge cases, no discarded maps, no secret orders in code, no tins of Bully Beef. Only patches of rough concrete and empty Nissen Huts with white-washed stones at the doors and metallically echoing interiors marked the recent military occupation. Some of the huts were usable and that was fortunate for our camp, as it was a wet, windy week in July.

The hut I had touched was intermittently live as a loose electric cable dangled down and scraped across it in the breeze. The shock hit me on the elbow's funny bone like a blow from a hammer. It flung me sideways and I landed on my back in the grass, elbow tingling, winded and frightened but happy to be alive. None of my friends would believe me that the hut was live but neither was anyone brave enough to touch it to prove that it was not.

We found the Clogmore Stone quite easily after what seemed a long and steep hike up through the forest. To my great surprise the stone was exactly where it was supposed to be on the map. It was a huge, erratic boulder left as one of nature's monuments by a retreating Ice Age. It was perched on the hill-side above the forest with a wonderful panoramic view of Carlingford Lough.

We could see across the lough to the mountains on the Cooley Peninsula in neutral Eire and the town of Omeath, well-known for its smuggling trade to Northern Ireland. Such was its fame that even in Belfast we had heard tales of small boats laden with day-trippers and contraband, chugging their way across the lough from Omeath. The little boats brought back bacon, butter, real pork sausages, sugar, nylons, cigarette lighters, chocolate, anything in short supply or rationed in the North from the land of plenty in the South.

Our camp was beside the little resort of Rostrevor on the shore of Carlingford Lough. A narrow street led to the broad, leafy square which was the heart of the village. To boys from the city, it was a quiet place, empty of people and, except at certain fixed times of day, almost completely silent. Its people were friendly, they were interested in us without intruding and always helpful. Although we were aware that this was a mainly Catholic village, everyone seemed pleased to have a Boys' Brigade company camping on their doorstep.

After so many years why do we remember some incidents so clearly and forget seemingly more important happenings so completely? Laurens Van Der Post believes that the African bushmen know. It is the feeling and the quality of the memory which is important, not the quantity or the exactness. Van Der Post calls this memory 'a compass for man in his search for truth'.

Is memory like religious belief, in that, unless we can be sure of the precise details others will deem it invalid? For me the true essence of remembering is simply the impression that this is the way it was. As if to remember an experience we must have truly felt it.

The night we scared ourselves with talk of ghosts was my first night in a tent. The bugler had blown 'Last Post' and 'Lights Out' had been called. The white Bell Tents were in a neat row, the doors closed with rope and toggles on the inside. For the first time that day the camp was quiet.

Each squad had its own tent and we lay on palliasses filled with straw, heads pointing outwards, feet towards the pole, like the spokes of a wheel. We had been shown how to fold our two blankets carefully and secure them with large blanket pins to form a sleeping bag. My pillow was my shoes padded with my shirt and trousers.

Rostrevor

The palliasse straw rustled and squeaked as we twisted around, jostling each other, trying to find a comfortable way to lie. We were tired but too excited to think of sleep. We were wary too, having heard tales of night raids when one squad would let down another's tent or hit a bump on the canvas with one of the wooden mallets used for driving in the tent pegs.

Silence was supposed to be the rule after 'Lights Out' so we had to talk very quietly. Someone said that this would be a good place to tell a ghost story and bravely we all agreed.

One of the older boys told us that he had been evacuated, a few years earlier, to his great aunt's house in the country. There the ghost of a woman wandered through the trees at night shaking the branches.

The woman was a neighbour and she had been on her way home from church one Sunday evening in the autumn when she was attacked by a gipsy. He had left her badly injured and dying but, in spite of the noise and her screams for help, no one from his aunt's house had come to her aid.

Narrow Water Castle

Now she came back to haunt them every year just before Christmas. She hid in the trees and howled and when they ventured out to look she rattled the branches to let them know she was there.

He told the tale as if he believed every word of it. It was a long story punctuated by pauses so quiet we could hear each other breathing. By the end we were all quite still with fear. Every rustle and swish of twigs in the breeze could have been herself come to torment us.

There was no more talking and no use any of us pretending to feel un-afraid. Even the teller had scared himself into silence, as if telling the tale had made it real.

I seemed to lie awake for a long time, curled up with the blanket covering the top of my head, leaving only my face free, trying not to hear the trees creaking.

The Boys' Brigade was founded in Scotland at the end of the last century. It is based on Christian principles, aiming to develop character and discipline and to give a sound religious training to boys from twelve to seventeen years of age. The officers were, and still are, volunteers and in our company all were committed born-again Christians. In Northern Ireland its companies are based at Presbyterian or Methodist churches. Our company was the 38th Belfast, attached to Donegall Road Methodist Church and was an important part of the life of that congregation.

The tradition of the Boys' Brigade Annual Camp began as a way to give city boys a cheap, active holiday in the open air. In our company the camp was a very special event and we saved for months towards its cost.

Our day began as the duty bugler sounded 'Reveille' at 8 a.m. In our uniforms of brown belts, and pill-box hats we formed ranks on parade for the raising of the flag and morning service. For special parades, like church service, the company band was on duty with bugles, side-drums and our company name on the big drum. On these occasions we wore our small, white haversacks which were the least popular item of equipment. Not only were they hard to keep clean but they served no purpose whatsoever except decoration. We wore a broad, highly-polished, brown leather belt with the BB crest as a buckle. The uniform was completed by a blue pill-box hat with white piping, a thin, patent leather strap and the number of our company, in chrome figures, on the front. There was skill involved in keeping this head gear on the head but, although it might well have looked odd and old-fashioned to others, we accepted it as normal.

After breakfast there was the tent and kit competition. The officers conducted an inspection, marks being allocated each day and a worthwhile prize for the best squad was awarded at the end of the week. That ended the formalities and, provided we were not late for meals or were not on kitchen duty, we were free to play games or find our own fun for the rest of the day.

Even at the take-it-all-for-granted age of thirteen, I was impressed by the dedication and patience of the officers. In later years at camp I saw how hard it was for them to control forty boys from the city, released temporarily from the discipline of home. Certainly the difficulties of mounting such a camp in war-time, coping with travel problems, food rationing and the shortage of camping equipment, must have made it a major undertaking. As I remember, the tents had to be hired from Black's of Greenock in Scotland, necessitating an order months ahead and the booking of freight space on the boat from Glasgow.

The officers even managed to provide a tuck shop with unlimited sweets at less than shop prices. Sweets and chocolate had been strictly rationed the previous year so this was a most welcome surprise. However, we did them the grave and ungrateful injustice of suspecting dealings on the black market. Our joking references to spivs and shady transactions must have been too hard for these honest men to bear. One morning at parade the Captain, who was obviously embarrassed and disappointed at having to explain, announced that the sweets were available because each of the officers had saved his sweet ration coupons for months and that the sweets and chocolate had been bought wholesale.

The truth was out but our officers were hurt because they had been forced to admit to, and thus appear to take credit for, such a generous act.

But it is for their introduction to living under canvas that I owe the BB officers their place in this tale. We erected the bell-tents with wooden pegs and great wooden mallets. It took some skill to pitch these big tents really well. The conical canvas had to be set just right. If the guy ropes were too slack or there were wrinkles in the canvas it would flap and crack in the wind. Too tight on the guys and the canvas might split as it shrank in the rain.

We had a cook with us whose job it was to feed over forty boys and men using an army field kitchen in the open air. We helped by preparing vegetables and washing up and my only memory of the food is that, in spite of rationing, there was always plenty for everyone.

Misdemeanours were punished by Fatigue Duties, which generally meant doing additional stints in the kitchen. Some tried to get their own back by bad-temperedly hacking most of the potato away with the skin but their pile of spuds when peeled, failed to fill the big dixies and they had to keep going until the the cook decided that there were enough.

There was no sense of rivalry between the Boys' Brigade and the Boy Scouts in our part of Belfast, probably because there were no scout troops in the vicinity of the Donegall Road. We knew that scouts took their camping very seriously and regarded BB camps with disdain. They used smaller, lighter equipment than our bell tents and were supposed to be experts at camp craft and camp cooking.

However, such was the impression made on me by our camp at Rostrevor that no scout camp could have produced a more enthusiastic convert to the outdoor way of life than I became. It was of no consequence that our tents were big and cumbersome, each one probably weighing a hundredweight, that our pegs, mallets, palliasses and field kitchen were not designed to be carried in a rucksac. By the end of that week I had decided that I was a camper, that sleeping out in a tent was the way to enjoy the open air.

It was one of those grand moments when a decision is made which affects the future course of a life.

Since those days, Rostrevor has been the site of horrendous atrocities of guerilla war, but it remains one of the most pleasant and friendly villages in Ireland. After many visits over the years it is still in a favoured and grateful place in my memory, calm, welcoming, charming.

Other annual camps followed on the north coast of Ulster at Portstewart and Ballycastle. Our tents were even supplied with wooden floors, in two large half-circles which fitted together to form a drier but much harder surface to sleep on.

Although I was not aware of it at the time, the process had begun. The BB camp had followed the trips to the River Lagan as the second stage of a journey in search of the great outdoors. That journey continued before the war ended.

The Square — Rostrevor

CHAPTER 4

The Black Mountain

Earlier in the war I had been in parts of counties Antrim and Down as an evacuee and the BB camps had taken me to the Mountains of Mourne and the North coast. Now, back at home in Belfast, the Antrim Hills looked so near and inviting it seemed obvious that we should climb one of the peaks.

Choosing the Black Mountain was easy, it was the nearest peak, it looked the biggest and we knew its name. We were aware, however, that the real difficulty would not be the distance of the walk, nor would it be the height or steepness of the hill.

We picked a Saturday for the ascent and, when the decision was made, there were three of us, myself and my two closest friends, Walter and Harry, all in our early 'teens. Then two other boys asked to join us and to their surprise, we agreed. It was rare for us to welcome company on such expeditions but they must have been as aware as we were that, confronted with the main difficulty of the adventure, it would be better to have five in the party rather than three.

I lived at the end of a short terrace in the first house in Glenmachan Street, off the Donegall Road. A polished brass plate on the wall beside our front door announced....

'Nurse Slader, S.R.N.
State Registered Midwife'.

The street was relatively new and was the last of the many rows of small, neat terraces which reached outwards from the city to be halted only by the Bog Meadows. Although the lavatory was still in a little shed in the back yard they were the first houses in the immediate neighbourhood to have been built with a room for a bath. Being at the end of the terrace meant that our bathroom had a window on an outside wall which allowed the hot water vapour to escape. Other houses in the street lacked this advantage and condensation was such a problem that the bath was sometimes used only to store coal.

My mother's practice stretched from the Protestant Sandy Row to the Catholic Falls Road, so we lived at the centre of her work. It was a pleasant, respectable, keep-to-yourself street where the neighbours were friendly in a quiet, reserved fashion which suited my mother admirably.

She had come to the area first in the nineteen twenties as a widow with two teenage children and had been allocated a Corporation house on the other side of the sectarian border, near the Falls Road. Her Catholic neighbours were glad to have a maternity nurse in residence but the area became an IRA strong-hold and she and her children were ordered to leave simply because they were Protestants.

There were no Corporation houses available to rent on the Protestant side of the river but she managed to find the deposit and arranged a mortgage for a house in the newly-built terrace in Glenmachan Street. Later she married my father and I was born over twenty years after she had begun to rear her first family.

My mother had never told me about being put out of her Corporation house by the IRA. I only heard that story recently from my half-sister who remembered the incident vividly. After all those years since the twenties there was still surprise in her voice as she told me about being forced to leave their home and their good friends in the neighbourhood. However, my sister was probably less surprised fifty years later when history repeated itself and she was ordered out of her home in the north of the city for the same reason.

During The Troubles of the twenties my mother had an official pass which allowed her to attend patients during the hours of curfew. She explained that it had not been of much use when she arrived at a street where a mother-to be was in labour and the republican and loyalist gunmen were firing at each other from either end. Her trick then was to hold out, around the corner, her brown leather nurses bag with one hand and wait until the shoot-ing stopped. A voice from the other end of the street would shout,

'It's O.K. nurse. Come on ahead.'

Later when the baby had been born she would hold out her bag again at the front door of the house. The shooting would stop and a voice would call,

'Nurse! What is it, a boy or a girl?'

When she replied, there would be a little cheer from either end and she was free to leave the house to walk back home.

This was, of course, before the new Health Service had brought free medical treatment to all and I was aware that there was a good deal of unemployment in our part of Belfast. I remember asking my mother if she often had patients who could not afford to pay.

She smiled and then looked serious, as if it was an interesting question.

'The poor always pay their bills.' she said. 'I've never had a bad debt. It's the well-off who need watching and there are not too many of them around here. They won't forget to pay the doctor but they might need reminding to pay the nurse.'

She went on to tell me that she had a few families who were too poor to pay in cash at the time. However, when they received a present of eggs or a couple of chickens from relations in the country, one of the children would be sent to our house with half of the eggs or one of the fowl.

'It's important to take it when it's offered.' she said, 'Like all of us, they need to keep their self-respect. That way they remain your friends.'

Although she had not told me of being put out of her house, she had often mentioned how friendly her Catholic neighbours had been when she and her children lived near the Falls Road, and I knew too, that the mothers of that district had continued to be her patients until she retired.

My four friends and I set off to climb the Black Mountain quite early. To reach the peak we would follow the route of the mis-called Yellow Convoy to the Falls Road and along the Whiterock Road to the foot of the hills. We would have to leave the gable-wall paintings of King Billy, cross The Blackie Bridge and pass under the IRA's golden instruction to silence.

When it is necessary to venture into a place which may be unwelcoming or even somewhat dangerous, it may be worth taking precautions and proceeding warily but it is never helpful

The Journey Beyond The Black Mountain

to talk too much about what might happen. So we set out, fears unspoken, walking quickly, talking when we had to in low voices.

We crossed the Blackie Bridge, passed the Match Factory and took a short cut up one of the streets which led to the Falls Road. At first it was empty, then a boy about our own age spotted us. He fled into an entry and we knew that it was to alert the boys of the neighbourhood. It was not a time to linger and, by the time he had spread the word and a mob of the lads had been assembled, we were out of realistic chasing distance.

The hostilities of the Bog Meadows War had not resumed on the scale of the earlier daily battles, but there were occasional skirmishes between teenage boys in Protestant or Catholic gangs. Both sides were always on guard and our main worry had been that we would be spotted far enough away to enable an ambush to have been set up. By going through the heart of the enemy's territory, quietly and quickly, we had taken them by surprise. The boys in the mob had to content themselves by shaking their fists, roaring insults and shouting threats about what they would do to us on our way back. From the safe distance of the top of the street we laughed and strode onwards, elated that our tactics had given us clear passage.

No one paid any attention to us as we crossed the Falls Road and followed the Whiterock Road to the foot of the hills. There was a spring in the lane which led out on to the mountain and we stopped to drink. It was called The Fountain and supposed to be the best water in Belfast. Having tasted it with suitable seriousness, we agreed.

When we reached the Hatchet Field it was hard to believe that this was it. From below it was the clearest of land-marks, the huge shaft and blade were bounded by hedges as if specially planted to make the shape. Now we were almost at the end of the farmland but from where we stood it was impossible to see the outline of the hatchet.

This was where the trekkers came on nights when air-raids were expected. I imagined a great crowd of people sheltering from the wind and rain under the hedges, families huddled together, watching the German aircraft fire-bombing their city. The scars were still there below us, great gaps where once homes and factories had been packed like potatoes in a clamp. Some of the flattened areas were huge, where a whole district had been devastated, but there were other little pockets where a single bomb had picked out one home for destruction and left its neighbours standing. When it was happening in 1942 I had been too young to understand, but not now. I stood and looked at the city in a trance, feeling that I now knew what war was like.

The others had left me behind and I walked quickly to catch up or to hurry away from an horrific past, suddenly revealed to me for the first time.

If there had been a vague feeling of disappointment with the Hatchet Field for not being more like our idea of it, when we came out on to the top of the Black Mountain, it was a reward beyond all expectations. It was not just the fact that the uphill slog was over. Nor was it the achievement of reaching the summit of a mountain. Over the years the apparent lack of importance to me, of this particular incentive for climbing mountains, has been intriguing.

It was confirmed a few years later when I went with a school friend called John, now a professor of medicine, to the Mourne Mountains for the first time. In two wonderful walking trips in winter conditions, each lasting four or five days, John and I never thought to climb a peak except on one occasion when we needed to see the next part of our route. At the time I was not aware of the absence of this desire to get to the top of every peak. For us the adventure was in finding our way through the mountains. We were there for the journey.

As the five of us stood on the top of the Black Mountain, our reward too was to be in this particular place, perched above the world as we knew it and with its details set out like tiny models on a gigantic map.

To the left was Belfast Lough, intruding between the uplands of Antrim and the very much lower hills of Down. Part of the city was obscured by a layer of smoke lying on it like a dark grey war-time blanket. It is easy to forget how necessary it was to have the clean air legislation and how effective it has been in an industrial city like Belfast.

Directly below us, where the Bog Meadows pushed its way into the city, the air was as clear as it was over the fields of the countryside. At the edge of the Meadows we could see the streets in which we lived and to our great satisfaction they were in this wedge of clean air, only just perhaps, but still in the clear.

We picked out the football grounds. Windsor Park, the home ground of Linfield Football Club, 'the wee blues', was beside the railway line and easily identified. It was the loyalists' team and had enormous support.

Celtic Park was very close to where we lived. It was the home of a famous team which, a few years later, was disbanded at its peak. Its colours were green and white and it was supported, although an occasional Protestant player played for the club, almost exclusively by Catholics.

Such was the sectarian support for these two great teams that every game between them brought the possibility of serious trouble. At one match it erupted so violently the directors of the Belfast Celtic Football Club decided that the only way to avoid further trouble was to stop playing. In a few weeks the most successful football team in Ireland had been disbanded and the club closed.

My father had encouraged me to support a third local team whose much less-glamorous ground was behind the houses of Roden Street. Even then I could understand his motives and accepted his lead.

Distillery Football Club was in the same league as Linfield and Celtic but was much less successful on the field of play. They played in white jerseys and lacked the star players and mass support of Linfield and Celtic. But my father's ploy worked and I remained a supporter of 'the whites' throughout my teens. This was in spite of the strongest pressure of friends and the attraction of another code of football at which I had some success as a school-boy player.

From our viewpoint it was easy to follow the course of the River Lagan. In the distance of the countryside to our right, the river twisted gently to the outskirts of the city, then vanished under the smokey cover, leaving us to guess where it flowed into the lough. Upstream we thought we could see our special place above Shaw's Bridge where we had collected fallen twigs and made a fire for roasting potatoes.

Such was our sense of wonder that it took time to take it all in. The problem of safe passage through foreign territory was almost forgotten. Now we would have a real tale to tell on our return. We were about to set off down the mountain, when someone suggested the we should go to the other side of the summit to see the view.

It was a good day for seeing into the distance, probably the kind of Irish day when the threat of showers seems to clear the air right back to the horizon.

Beyond the Black Mountain there was a huge prospect before us, the countryside of our country. Londonderry-Antrim-Down-Armagh-Tyrone-Fermanagh. I could hear the sing-song rhyme of Northern Ireland's counties ringing in my head, the way we had chanted them aloud at Broadway Public Elementary School.

Could we see them all from here? Now we might understand why we had been forced to learn Geography at school. Here it was, the real thing, the shape of the land laid out in front of us. It made sense of even the dullest of lessons.

Lough Neagh, the biggest lake in the British Isles looked so close. Teachers of Geography seemed to be keen on 'the biggest'. In those days Belfast was supposed to have the biggest single shipyard in the world, Harland and Wolff, and the Belfast Ropeworks was also claimed to be the biggest in the world.

Facts like these we knew, because information had been such an important part of our education. However, until this moment, knowing about Lough Neagh meant little when we had never seen a lake much larger than a pond. But here it was, the biggest lake in the British Isles. We were impressed. It was huge. It was most certainly an enormous lake.

The Antrim Hills rolled gently away to the north and only one peak stood out. It was fairly close and seemed higher. It could only have been Divis. On the other side of Lough Neagh were the Sperrins and in the far distance we were sure we could see the Hills of Donegal. It took time to sort it all out but, instead of the usual arguing between us, for some reason it was easy for all five of us to agree on what we could identify.

We decided that we could see five of the six counties. Sweeping around in a clockwise direction lay Down, Armagh, Tyrone, Londonderry and Antrim. Without knowing why, it seemed to me to be a most significant discovery, one of the most important events in my life. And at that moment I made a decision.

I told the others that, if we wanted to see the world, the obvious place to start was our own country. They were interested and we quickly agreed that, as soon as we were allowed to go, we would load up our bicycles and cycle around Northern Ireland.

It was such an exciting idea that the view and the effort of the walk to the summit and even our foray through enemy territory were now in the back of our minds.

We had no intention of returning home by the way we had come in case the mob was still waiting for us on the sound but incomplete logic that we would have to return sometime. We crossed the Blackie further upstream by a foot-bridge and arrived at the street corner which was the parting of our ways, flushed with success.

Our enthusiasm was not matched by that of our parents; the only one who seemed quietly in favour was my father. We had to wait until the war was over before we could begin the expedition. The parents had good reasons against such a foolhardy trip. Rationing was still strictly in force. Spare parts for bicycles were scarce and expensive. With the threat of invasion early in the war, many road signs had been removed and had yet to be replaced. It seems hard to believe now, in these days of organised Duke of Edinburgh Award Expeditions and school trips to the ski slopes, but the biggest difficulty then, was that this was an entirely new idea to our parents.

How would we find our way? How could we carry all our equipment on our bicycles? Where would we stay? What if something went wrong and we were miles from home?

We did our best to persuade them and prepared in secret. We used a road map to plan the route and tried to guess how far we might cycle in a day.

Heading west through County Down would bring us to Armagh. We would turn north on the far side of Lough Neagh, through counties Tyrone and Derry and reach the north coast. Turning right again we would follow the coast along the north of County Antrim and that would bring us to Fair Head and the north-east corner of the island. Following the shore would take us south along the Antrim Coast Road and back home to Belfast.

It was about 200 miles and it seemed a very long way. How many days would it take? The furthest any of us had ridden was less than ten miles. We tried and failed to find out how far a person could cycle in a day. In the end we decided to allow about five days.

We went for a practice run one evening along the road to Lisburn, but had to turn back a short way beyond the city limits because it was late. It was the first time so many of us had gone together for a ride of any distance. It took a collision between two of us, and an argument about who was at fault, to convince us that that we needed to agree who would lead and who would follow.

As a trial run, it was disappointing but, in spite of the collision, we had hilarious fun. Indeed we laughed so much on the way back that one of the boys lost control and wet himself as he cycled along.

Later in life he became a prominent Unionist politician and our cycle run must have taught him something about the dangers of enjoying himself too much in a public place.

In the event, only two of us were allowed to go. Optimistic noises from the others were silenced by mothers who thought that the whole idea of the trip was reckless. Some of the other fathers may have approved, but if so, they kept their ideas to themselves. We were of an age and this was at a time, when mothers often took the responsibility for deciding such matters, on the principle, that if they were expected to take charge of the purse strings and to provide the day-to-day discipline for the family, they were also in charge of all important affairs.

My mother allowed herself to be persuaded. I knew it was causing her considerable heart searching but she must have understood how important it was for me to go. My father said very little, but I knew he was in favour and guessed that he was arguing the case out of my hearing. His way was to produce, as a present, some small but important item, like the map or a piece of camping gear, without comment but as a clear token of support.

The other boy, who was allowed to go, was called Stanley and he was the youngest of our group, about thirteen years of age. His mother was young and very pretty and probably thought that being nearly a year or so older, I would look after him.

CHAPTER 5

The Lambeg Drum

The three friends, who were not allowed to go with us, were disappointed and resentful. At that age it hurt the pride, when your mother refused to agree that you could go, where your friends were allowed to go. To their great credit, however, instead of turning against the trip and making fun of us for attempting it, as sour grapes might have dictated, they decided to help us.

One managed to borrow a most essential article for us, a light-weight ridge tent. It was small, white, and very flimsy. We were used to the substantial canvas of the big BB bell-tents and were doubtful of the waterproof or stormproof qualities of this little shelter. However, our thanks were genuine. Without a tent, light enough for us to carry, the trip would have had to be cancelled.

At BB camp we had two blankets each, but when we looked at the bulk of two blankets, rolled as tightly as we could manage, we decided that one each would have to do.

My mother lent me a small methylated spirit stove. It was only a few inches high with three fragile metal legs on which to set a pot. Its spirit reservoir was as wide as a small saucer and had a wire-mesh grid at the top. She told me we would have to eat well to have enough energy for the cycling, but explained that it would not matter if we were not able to cook much for the few days of the trip, as long as we had plenty to eat.

On the morning we left home the packing started early at my house, where the equipment was stored. It was a long and complicated operation. Stanley and I shared out the gear and food. As well as the tent and stove we had two very light cooking pots, a strong bottle filled with methylated spirit and a waterproof ground-sheet.

In spite of very strict rationing, the assembled food looked impressive. Although we were at peace now, some rations were at a lower level than during the most difficult days of the war.

Very recently, bread had been added to the list. However, boys of our age were allowed about half as much again as an adult and the problem was not the size of the ration but the fact that we could only carry a small amount with us and would have to bring bread coupons to be able to buy more.

At that time the standard rations for one person for one week were ...

8 ozs. sugar	2 ozs. bacon
3 ozs. butter	4 ozs. jam
3 ozs margarine	2 ozs. cheese

$2^1/2$ ozs. tea (for an adult, less for a child)
9 bread units for an adult, 13 for an 11–18 year-old
(1 unit = 7 ozs. bread)

Our stores included a large, white loaf which was the most bulky and awkward item to pack. There was a pound of bacon rashers carefully wrapped in grease-proof paper. This was the full ration for two people for four weeks. We had butter and jam in screw-topped jars, sugar, tea and salt, a half pint of milk in a bottle with a stopper, a tin of meat and a dark grey, waxed carton of American Lease-Lend dried eggs. Lease-Lend was an American scheme for supplying munitions and food to her allies and the dried eggs were greatly appreciated, but only by those who had discovered how to cook them properly.

Near the top we packed sandwiches and about two weeks rations of sweets and chocolate to keep us going.

We had a road map, which I insisted on carrying, a candle, two boxes of matches and a tin opener. Each of us had a little money tied up in the corner of his handkerchief. Then, of course, there were the bread coupons and Stanley was allowed to take charge of them.

As we were packing in the street in front of our house we heard the fish man calling from the next street.

'Herrins – a – lough – oi!.... Herrins – a – lay!'

My friends and I had worked out what he meant, although it had taken time and much argument.

It was ... 'Herrings from Lough Neagh.... Herrings alive.'

He pushed his hand cart piled with gleaming, silvery fish and slivers of ice into our street still calling loudly and with effortless ease.

My mother smiled. My father and I liked our herrings fried but she was very fond of a potted herring. She often kept a few in our safe. In the days before a refrigerator became one of the basic necessities of life, the safe was the little cabinet with wire-mesh sides which hung outside on the the north-facing wall of our yard. Herrings were a shilling (5p) per dozen then, although our fish man always gave thirteen to the dozen. Not only did my mother think they were good value, she made sure I knew that fish was one of the most nutritious of foods.

'Pity you couldn't take a few herrings with you.' she said. 'But then you'll be going by Lough Neagh itself and there should be no shortage of fish there.'

We each packed a knife, fork, spoon and an enamel plate and mug. Although we were unconvinced that they were necessary for such a short trip, discretion required us to include towels, soap, tooth brushes and tooth paste.

The tent was securely tied to the carrier of my bicycle. We tried to fit everything else into our saddle bags and the small haversacks that we intended to carry on our backs. The blankets were so bulky they almost defeated our best efforts but eventually my mother produced a strip of waxed cloth and with one tightly rolled in this and the other protected by the ground sheet, they too, were eventually tied in place.

Feeling slightly self-conscious, we said our good-byes, first at my home where the packing had drawn a small, silent audience and then to his mother, as his house was on our route.

After the first fifty yards a boy we knew, but who was not a friend, shouted something insulting after us. It sounded like,

'Neee-eet-root', called in a silly, sing-song lilting voice, with each phrase held like the call of the fish man.

We knew what he meant. The previous year he had been a member of a gang of boys who had captured Stanley and me because we were wearing school uniforms. They were the only two school uniforms in the district and were regarded by some of our peers as a form of provocation. When I went to grammar school and played rugby for the first time, I discovered that it was

DUNLUCE
CASTLE

BALLYCASTLE

PORTRUSH

COLERAINE

ANTRIM
HILLS

MAGHERA

LARNE

SPERRIN
MOUNTAINS

LOUGH
NEAGH

THE
BLACK
MOUNTAIN

BELFAST

BALLYCLOG
CHURCH

COALISLAND

LISBURN

PORTADOWN

LURGAN

B.S.

MOURNE
MOUNTAINS

ROSTREVOR

The Journey Beyond The Black Mountain

regarded by the teachers and most of the pupils as a rough, tough game. It was no more so than wearing a school uniform, at that time, in some parts of Belfast.

The gang had tied us to a fence and announced that we were to be washed with a cabbage leaf dipped in a puddle and then painted with a rotten beetroot they had found in a refuse bin. In a red mist of rage, which had nothing to do with bravery, I broke free and scattered them with one of the brush shafts which were this gang's weapons. The brush shaft broke across the abdomen of one of the bigger boys and he screamed in pain. Once he was released, Stanley flung himself into the battle like a terrier after rats and the gang fled before us.

I threw the broken pieces of the brush shaft over the fence to which we had been tied and felt no elation at winning the battle, only anger at the attempted humiliation. That evening we heard that the boy I had hit had been taken to hospital. Until he was released a few days later, I discovered what it was to feel real anxiety, without being able to share my fears.

The incident had the effect of ensuring safe passage for us from then on, in the immediate neighbourhood and I suppose it helped me to develop a degree of physical self-confidence, which every teenage boy has need of and which, if it does not develop at this age, can dog the man for the rest of his life. However, the violence of my own reaction made me wary of street fights, in case someone might be badly injured and I might be responsible.

'Neet-root!' the boy called again, not quite so loudly. He was less sure of himself now we had stopped to watch him. Stanley and I laughed at his insult and pretended to turn our bikes to chase him. He ran off and we were properly on our way.

The embarrassment of riding bicycles laden with gear like pack mules faded as we pedalled up the little slope of Tate's Avenue Bridge and over the railway line. We reached the road to Lisburn in great good humour, laughing at the fun we had had on the evening of the practice ride.

At the King's Hall, on the outskirts of the city, we saluted the spot where our friend had chuckled himself into our private history, as the lad who could do four things at once..... laugh until he cried, ride a bicycle and relieve himself..... all at the same time.

The road through the suburbs was lined with pleasant houses, each with its neat front garden and trees. We had been this far before on our walks and regarded it as one of those places which only the well-off could afford. To us, it was second only to the Malone Road, where the very wealthy lived.

I felt no envy what-so-ever, our house in Glenmachan Street had everything a home needed except a garden and we had the biggest garden in Belfast, the Bog Meadows, at the top of the street. As well as that, to live here in the suburbs would mean being away from the Donegall Road and my friends and the BB and the centre of the world as I knew it.

The village of Finaghy seemed attached to Belfast by the unbroken line of houses on either side of the road, but a little farther on Dunmurray was larger, longer, a separate, self-contained place, with shops like a small town.

Lambeg's houses were not much in evidence from the road, but there was a railway station. We pretended that we were exhausted after the 5 miles we had managed so far and jokingly discussed taking the train back home.

It was a surprise to find Lambeg such a quiet place. For me it was a name I associated only with the name of the massive drum, the Orangeman's Lambeg Drum. Even now I can hear its wild, deep, booming roar throbbing across the summer night air of the city.

During the week before the Orangemen marched on their Twelfth of July parade, there were Lambeg Drum playing competitions. The nearest took place in Sandy Row more than a mile away but, such was the volume of sound, it might have been coming from the next street.

The drums were played by stocky, huge-stomached men, jackets off, collars and ties discarded, sleeves rolled to the elbows. The drum was carried by a leather strap around the back of the neck, the drummer leaning well back to get the balance. It was as big in diameter as the big drum of a marching band but it was twice as thick and obviously very much heavier. Only the skin of a goat was tough enough, it was reckoned, and there was a goat farm in County Down which specialised in producing the special skins.

It was a hard man's drum, they said. Many a tough character was not even able to walk upright with the weight of it around the neck. The drummers had forearms like Popeye and battered the skins with thick springy canes, one in each fist. They played in

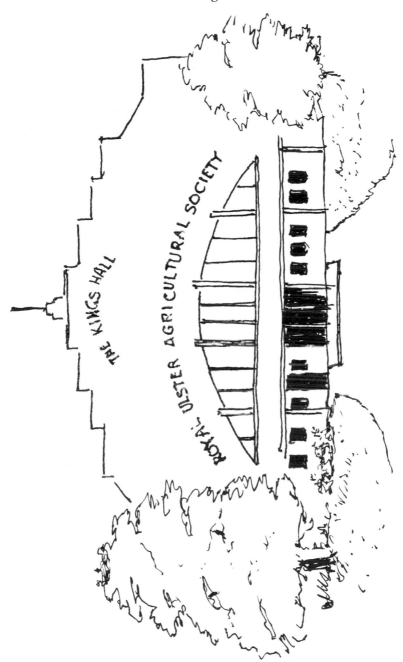

THE KINGS HALL

ROYAL ULSTER AGRICULTURAL SOCIETY

pairs, their faces red, blotched with purple. Their necks bulged to bursting, one trying to drum the other off the street.

The rhythms were stylised, in recognisable patterns, booming and crashing like big waves on a rocky shore. Each drummer flailed on in a trance, willing his own beat to dominate and blast the other out of hearing and out of sight. The noise rose in a crescendo until it filled the air and the head with sound. It was unlike any beat I knew except the African drums I had heard at the cinema. It was primitive, elemental, like a vast horde of nimble Zulu giants dancing. It was a war drum, beaten to strike terror in the hearts of the enemy.

To Catholic ears it must have been a hated sound, arrogant, intimidating, provocative, the arch symbol of Protestant Triumphalism. There was no escape from it, except by leaving the country. On certain nights in July its booming roar would have rolled across the whole city and filled the air with hostile vibration in villages and towns around the countryside.

The Lambeg Drum

Without wondering why, many Protestants would have felt the wee hairs on the back of the neck rising with excitement. For them, it was the most powerful evocation of their cause, more potent than brilliantly coloured gable-wall pictures of King William on his white charger. The visual arts may stimulate the mind and touch the spirit but sound rouses the deepest of our primitive emotions. The Lambeg Drum was the very essence of 'No Surrender'.

But there were no signs of tribalism as Stanley and I passed the village of Lambeg, no flags, or bunting or kerb-stones painted red, white and blue or sounds of flute and drum. They would come later in the month.

Beyond the village the road was busy with traffic and we had been warned to be careful. Such was the number of vehicles using this road that when major road developments were being planned some years later, this stretch between Belfast and Lisburn was chosen as the first full-scale motorway to be constructed in the United Kingdom.

However, heavy traffic is relative and at the time of our trip there was only one tenth of the vehicles on Northern Ireland's roads that there are now.

As we pushed our way towards Lurgan, the haversacks became so uncomfortable and tiring that we had to stop. It seemed foolish to be carrying this load on our backs and in desperation we lashed them to the pile we each had behind our saddles. It was a wonderful relief to be able to pedal without the weight on the shoulders and we fancied ourselves as the first to have discovered that cyclists should let the cycle frame do the carrying. To my amazement I still see cyclists struggling along with loaded ruck-sacs on their backs. Their friends should tell them to let the cycle frame take the strain.

Every few miles we paused to study the map. We passed the village of Magheralin near which my mother had been born. I remembered visiting my cousins there before the war, mainly because they had given me nettle soup at dinner time. At the time I had thought they were making fun of me and insisted that someone else taste the soup before me. When I tried it, to my great surprise, my tongue was not stung. The soup was delicious. My aunt also made champ, one of my favourite meals, a traditional

Lurgan

Ulster dish of potatoes creamed with butter, but instead of fla-
vouring the champ with chopped scallions, or spring onions, she
added nettles which had been boiled and shredded.

Back home, no one but my mother would believe me when I
told them about the wonderful nettle soup and the nettle champ.

We entered the wide main street of Lurgan and rode slowly
towards the large church at the other end. It was unfamiliar, even
though I must have visited it many times when I was an evacuee
in nearby Waringstown. The town dates back to the reign of James
1 and had an impressive air of spacious, country grandeur.

A few miles further, Portadown seemed to have been laid out
by the same town planner. Although, in the 17th century, when
Lurgan was a town Portadown was still a village at a ford across
the River Bann. However, when the Newry canal was opened in
1741, Portadown soon became a prosperous town, linked by that
canal to the sea at Carlingford Lough. A little later, the Lagan
Canal was opened and this meant that, by using Lough Neagh,
boats could ply their trade between Portadown and Belfast.

Portadown

Portadown too, had a very broad main street, with a church at the far end, although this church had a solid, square-based tower rather than a spire. We speculated about the reasons for a church having a spire or a tower. Was it for defence or because of the size of its bells? Was one Church of Ireland and the other Presbyterian?

Beyond the town we were immediately amongst the orchards, cycling through rolling countryside where the hills were gentle and, for the first time, we could see for miles.

The route which seemed shortest went close by Washing Bay on Lough Neagh, but it looked, on the map, as if there was no bridge at the mouth of the Blackwater River and we would have to depend on there being a ferry. We were aware too, that the road signs, which had been removed during the war, might not have been replaced. We chose instead the road to Coalisland and covered the miles easily. It was as if we had turned away from the traffic into the real countryside and, when a car or a lorry passed, the driver waved.

The map had to be consulted frequently because of the shortage of road signs and we had to make a number of crucial turns. We came upon a strange, spongy, gently undulating road which carried us across a stretch of bog land and past a lake. When a car or a lorry passed the road seemed to tremble as if it was floating on the bog.

There was no sign of Lough Neagh, but we knew it must be close on our right and we had come far enough to swing around to its far side. Having started in County Antrim, we had crossed into County Down near Lurgan. Before Portadown our route had entered County Armagh and now, still on our first day, we were in County Tyrone.

The road was empty, so we gave ourselves three cheers and pedalled easily northwards into the late afternoon.

CHAPTER 6

'Four Counties in a Day!'

'Four counties in a day!' The sound of it rang out along the empty road as we shouted to each other, using different voices, saying it with degrees of seriousness, like actors repeating a phrase for emphasis, making sure the audience understood the full significance of what had been said.

Once through Coalisland, we discussed the name. Did it really mean that the town was on an island where coal could be mined? We agreed that the settlement might well have been built on an island in the river, but scoffed at the very idea of coal mining. Everyone knew, we told each other, that there were no coal mines in Northern Ireland, that all our coal had to be imported. Had we but asked, we might have discovered that coal, in the form of lignite, has indeed been mined in this area from time to time over the years.

On the way to Moneymore, we decided that we had come far enough for one day and should find a place to camp. On the left-hand side of the road there was a ruin of an ancient church, which we discovered later was called Ballyclog. Almost opposite, on the other side of the road, was another church of unusual design, with a high, steeply-pitched roof. It looked old too, but not so ancient as the ruin and it seemed to be still in use. Supporting the outside wall and the roof was a type of curved stone arch which I had seen before only as an illustration in a book. It must be a flying buttress, the one architectural term I knew and remembered solely because it was so imaginatively named.

However, the most dramatic feature was a tall spire, rising from ground level at the front of the church. It was built like an Irish round tower but more elegant, narrower, rising steeply, sloping inwards to support the building and capped with the sharpest spire I had ever seen.

It was such a contrast to our own church in Belfast that we

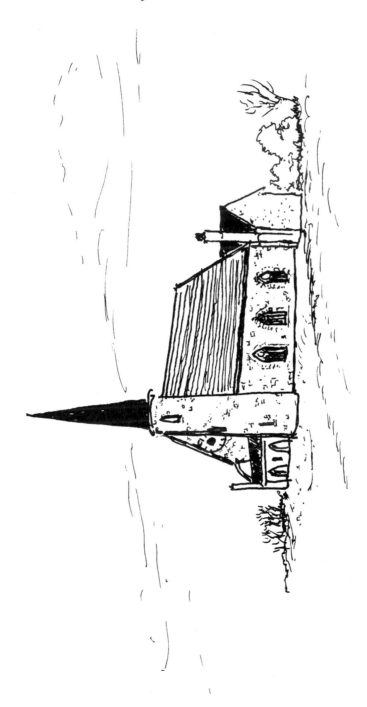

Ballyclog Church

stopped to look. To me it was more like a handsome fortification than a place of worship. Donegall Road Methodist Church was relatively new and was probably one of the finest Protestant churches in the city. It was large, functional and set at the centre of its congregation. Inside, it was spacious, bright and airy, decorated in light colours and furnished in well-polished wood, with pews, pulpit and a large balcony on three sides.

Its predecessor must have had a corrugated iron roof, as local Presbyterians and others still called it the 'Tin Tap' to make sure the members of its congregation did not get above themselves, now that they had a grand new church.

Stanley and I were cycling slowly and it was easier to talk to each other. The road wound its way over and around little hills and between the thick hedges. Now, this whole countryside seems built over with neat new houses and bungalows, each on its own plot, separated from its neighbours by a field or two. Then, it was a quiet country road with a few farm dwellings tucked behind big bushes.

We met a man fixing a fence and stopped to ask him about a place to camp. He smiled and greeted us pleasantly, asking questions in a slow precise way and in an accent we had never heard before. He had a countryman's curiosity, inquisitive but trying to hide his surprise at meeting us here.

'Where were we from? What were we doing here? Who did we know in this townland? Why were two city boys touring in the wilds of County Tyrone?'

It was our first conversation with anyone other than each other since early morning and we were pleased to have someone so friendly to talk to.

He was a wiry build of a man, of medium height, dressed in dark clothes. His face showed his interest but, by the way he talked, he was not a man who could be too serious for too long.

When I had been evacuated to the country during the war, I had learned that, when it was important to have the right answer from a countryman, it was never a good idea to ask the question too soon or too directly.

I felt that convention had been observed. We had come a long way and were very tired. It was time to ask about a place to camp. I told him that we had a small tent and were looking for somewhere to pitch it. I asked him if he knew of anyone nearby who would give us permission to put the tent up for one night.

'It'll rain.' he said, looking at the skyline. 'There'll be heavy rain before morning.'

'It's all right.' said Stanley speaking for the first time and with the confidence of youth that made the man grin. 'The tent will keep us dry.'

The farmer looked at us in in a very deliberate way, sizing us up.

'Maybe so.' he said kindly. 'But if your wee tent is small enough to be in those packs,' and he nodded at the gear on the backs of our bicycles, 'It'll be so flimsy the rain will spit through it.'

The tent certainly was light and we had yet to spend a night in it or even put it up, but the farmer's lack of confidence in its ability to withstand bad weather failed to worry us.

He gathered up his tools and began to walk away, with a look over his shoulder which meant we were to follow. After a short distance, he turned into a lane between high hedges. I walked behind him on legs that felt like rubber but glad to be walking for a change. Now I was out of the sitting position I felt the saddle soreness. Stanley saw me rub the tender spot and nodded in sympathy. We said nothing, in case the man might hear. Some discomforts are best suffered in silence.

We turned a bend in the lane and came upon a farmhouse at the far side of a farm yard. The man pointed in the direction of the house.

'Try him.' said our friend, 'He's as decent a man as you'll find around here.'

The lane continued around the house and he walked away with a cheery wave. We shouted our thanks after him, propped the bikes against each other and I knocked with my knuckles on the door.

It was opened by a pleasant woman in a large, floral apron, with flour on her hands. I was expecting the farmer himself to appear and had been rehearsing to myself what I would say, with this in mind. She seemed a kindly lady, but the words refused to come. I looked around and Stanley was standing by the bicycles, wondering what I was up to.

'Yes?' The woman said the word so lightly and gently that I was immediately at ease.

'We're looking for a place to pitch our tent for the night.' I said, forgetting all my good intentions not to ask too soon or too directly.

'We met a man down at the road fixing a fence and he said that you might give us permission.'

The woman wrinkled her forehead. I could almost hear her wondering who this man might be. Suddenly she started forward as if given a push from the rear and our friend, the fence mender, was standing beside her.

'Who have you here?' he said, 'As soon as my back's turned you're entertaining travelling lads at the front door.'

She giggled and gave him a nudge with her elbow as if to tell him to behave himself.

'They want to camp.' she said 'Some character they met told them they could stay here. And so they can. They can use the orchard.'

'Oh, I don't know.' said the man. 'I'm not sure you'll be able to sleep easy in your bed with two city hooligans parked in the orchard.'

He shrugged his shoulders with a great show of resignation.

'But if that's what you want, go right ahead and let them. And on your own head be it.'

Stanley had come to join me and he and I watched this performance, mouths open, faces probably showing our bewilderment at this strange reversal of fortune, not knowing what to say next.

The woman, obviously the farmer's wife, gave her husband another dig in the ribs.

'Oh, give over.' she said to him, 'Stop teasing the boys and let them get their tent fixed.' She dusted the flour off her hands and nodded to us.

'Com'on.' she said 'Bring your bikes after me and I'll show you the orchard. If we don't move now he'll keep us here with his foolery all evening.'

She set off across the farmyard, chatting away as if she had known us all our lives.

The orchard was small and sheltered and seemed the most perfect camp site imaginable. The trees were laden with apples and there were wind-falls on the ground. The woman must have read our minds.

'They aren't ripe yet.' she said kindly, 'So it wouldn't do to try to eat them. If you come round to the kitchen later I'll find some good eaters for you.'

She left us on our own and we unpacked our gear in a higgle-de-piggledy heap. The tent was pitched with less trouble than expected but it looked small and, as the man had predicted, very flimsy. The ground-sheet almost covered the space inside and we laid our blankets side by side to make it look comfortable. The food and equipment were carefully arranged around the sides but not close enough to touch the canvas.

From our camping with the Boys' Brigade we knew that to touch the wet canvas when it is raining will cause the tent to leak. This vital fact of camp lore had been explained to us at the beginning of our first camp by an earnest officer. However, learning by precept alone is rarely the most effective educational method with boys of that age. On the next wet night, as we lay in our blankets on straw filled palliasses, four of us conducted a simple experiment by reaching up and poking the canvas above our heads.

All four spots began to drip steadily and we had to move our palliasses to let the drops fall between us rather than on our blankets.

Later I learned that that the leak might be diverted by drawing a finger down the canvas from the site of the drip to the ground. Unfortunately this technique for stopping a leak was never as effective as touching the canvas was in starting one.

Compared with the tarpaulin-like fabric of the bell-tents the material of our little white tent looked about as waterproof as a well-washed handkerchief. The BB camp was, what the outdoors books called, Fixed Camping and this was Light-weight Camping. Then, we had the comfort and protection of big tents and heavy equipment. Now, we had only what we could carry with us on our bicycles. Our trip would be not only a test of the gear we had brought, but of our ability to use it.

Once we had made camp we were in good spirits, this was the way to travel, to see the country, to go on an adventure. Already we had visited four of our six counties and had found a fine place to stay. Our small tent would be our home until the next day and we had pitched it ourselves.

That feeling of excitement and satisfaction, on having found a new place to make camp, recurs with agreeable frequency in my memory from that particular moment. I have come to see it as a manifestation of some primitive nomadic urge to find a safe haven. For me, being able to rest at night in safety and in some comfort wherever I happen to be, is an essential part of the journey. The locations have been magnificent, on the hills and islands of Ireland and in wild and remote places from the Arctic to the Himalayas. But this first camp in County Tyrone has a special place in my memories.

Stanley and I sat cross-legged inside the tent and studied the map. Carefully we measured our day's journey with a piece of string and reckoned that we had covered about fifty miles. It seemed a long way but we checked it again to see if we could make it a little longer.

When we set out on our journey, the inauguration of the Duke of Edinburgh Award Scheme was still ten years in the future. At the time, I was fifteen and Stanley was a year or so younger. It is intriguing to me now to realize that the distance we had done was similar to that decided as reasonable for boys a year or two older, on the first day of a Gold Award expedition by bicycle.

In the nineteen forties it would have been unusual for boys of our age to have undertaken such a journey. However, when the Award Scheme came to the Province in the late fifties, teachers and youth leaders encouraged it so successfully that walking and cycling expeditions for young people soon became popular. It happened to such an extent here that, as I write, a higher proportion of young people take part in the scheme in Northern Ireland than in any other part of the United Kingdom and indeed, no doubt reflecting the enthusiasm of their leaders, N.I. is the only part of the U.K. where more girls than boys take part.

Then, Stanley and I felt like pioneers, as if we might have been doing something quite new.

We planned the next part of the route, towards the north coast and on the strength of such a good start, decided that we need not travel so far on the second day.

We heard a shout of greeting and the farmer's head appeared in the doorway of the tent. He had brought us half a dozen apples.

'Come into the house for a cup of tea.' he said 'You won't want to be doing any cooking in here.'

We followed him into the kitchen and sat down with him at the fire. His wife gave us each a mug of sweet, milky tea and a large slice of apple tart on a plate. It took some doing to hold the mug in one hand and balance the plate on the knees, but we managed. It was our first food since the sandwiches at lunch time and neither of us refused a second slice.

The farmer and his wife took their ease by the open fire of carefully placed peats, obviously pleased that we were enjoying the home cooking. They asked us to come back for the evening meal and that was very tempting, but we had set out on our journey to try to look after ourselves. We told them that we had a spirit stove and they saw that we wanted to try to cook our own meal.

The farmer rose from the fire and showed us to an empty cottage across the yard.

'It'll be raining hard before long and you had best cook in here. Fetch your food and I'll bring you a shovelful of hot turf to start the fire. A good fire will be better for the cooking and you'll save the spirit for your stove.'

CHAPTER 7

The Spongy Road

He showed us to the barn where the peats were stored and we carried our arms full across to the cottage. We watched him make the fire, first with small pieces piled on the glowing lumps brought from the house, then I helped him with the long, narrow, slabs of hard, black turf.

Each piece was placed carefully, stacked neatly, pyramid fashion. He was impressed, as I seemed to know what to do, having worked with peat on the farm in North Antrim. There we had gone to the moss, as the bog was called, and the farmer had cut the soft, wet slabs in slow, easy rhythm. This was the skilled job and only he and his eldest son did it. They worked steadily, apparently without great effort although it must have required both strength and stamina. His younger son Billy and I had helped to stack the slabs for drying when they were ready.

Back at the farm there was a large Dutch barn piled with turf brought back from the bog and I remembered the harsh feeling of the turf when it was well dried, the surface rough enough to take the skin off hands not used to work.

As the smoke rose and the warmth permeated the kitchen, the cottage was transformed. On entering the room, it had felt cold, cheerless, as if it had been abandoned. Now, for a little while, it was a home again.

Outside, the clouds had closed in around the farm, threatening rain, but here we would be able to spend the evening in comfort, after our long day. Although we were only staying until the morning, it was our first night and we needed this easy, country hospitality far more than we realized at the time.

As he left us to go back to the house, the farmer shouted over his shoulder,

'Use as much of the turf as you need. There's no shortage of it in these parts.'

We had asked if we might buy some fresh milk and potatoes and in a few minutes he was back carrying a wicker basket with everything we had requested, as well as four eggs and a cabbage.

'You can pay before you leave in the morning.' he said 'I think I can trust you that far.' He winked so that we could be sure he was joking. I suspect that his wife had told him that it was not fair to tease these city boys too much.

The kitchen still had its wooden table and two old easy chairs. There was a large black kettle, an iron pan and a selection of pots which, by the look of them, had served a long time on the open fire. Above the fireplace was an iron beam, hung with chains and hooks. It was pivoted at one side so that it could be swung out from the fire and pots hooked to its chains.

We hung two pots half filled with water from the butcher's hooks, put the washed potatoes in one to boil in their skins and the cabbage in the other. We fried some of the bacon we had brought in its own fat. It was possible to do so then, in the days before bacon was injected with water to make it weigh heavier. When the cabbage was done and drained, we tossed it in the hot bacon fat, as I had seen my mother do at home.

By the time it was all cooked, we were ready. There was too much to put on our enamel plates at once, so we took it in stages. For a start, we had four potatoes each and a pile of cabbage, with rashers neatly arranged on top. Then we had the same again and that finished the bacon and cabbage.

The farmer had brought us a large can of milk, so we re-filled our enamel mugs. Almost absentmindedly, now we were in the mood for eating, we continued with the potatoes, taking one at a time and mashing it with a little butter. Not only was hunger assuaged, there was a profound feeling of satisfaction that we had been able to cook it by ourselves.

We put more turf on the fire and washed the dishes and pots in the huge sink. There was a knock on the door. It was not locked, but whoever was outside waited for us to open it. I lifted the latch and the top half of the door swung open.

'Visitors.' said the farmer's wife, who was carrying the wicker basket.

'Are you not going to ask us in for a cup of tea and a crack?' said the farmer. 'We brought our own mugs.' and he produced, from behind his back, two short, squat mugs in the traditional Ulster style.

The basket contained a large apple tart, a tea caddy and four delph plates. The farmer's wife placed them on the table. Stanley filled the black kettle and hung it on a hook over the fire.

'I see you know how to drive the crane.' said the farmer, pointing at the pivoted iron beam over the fire.

When the water boiled, his wife insisted that we use the tea from her caddy and save our own.

'You've a long way to go.' she said 'You might be glad of it before you reach home again.'

While the tea was brewing, she showed us how to light the lamp. She checked the wick to see that it was clean, then the level of paraffin. The wick had to be turned down once it was lit so that it burned with a blue flame. Stanley fitted the glass chimney and turned the wick up again, to fill the room with soft light.

'Mind you don't turn it too high.' she said anxiously, 'It'll smoke the chimney and we'll see nothing.'

The four of us sat in a semicircle around the fire, our two friends in the easy chairs and Stanley and I on upturned boxes.

Years later, I came down to a remote village, high in the mountains of Afghanistan. With a few friends, I was entertained to a meal by the Malik, the village head man, and we sat on a pile of carpets on the roof of his house, watching the blue of the peaks of the Hindu Kush deepen as the evening faded behind them.

So that we could talk on into the night in a circle of light, one of the Malik's sons brought a lamp and there was something familiar about its shape. I leaned it to one side and read the maker's name …

The Tilley Lamp Co. Ltd. Lisburn, Northern Ireland.

In our circle of light, in the cottage in Tyrone, the conversation rambled effortlessly along. The farmer and his wife were intrigued by the very idea of our journey and we told them about the day's trip.

When I mentioned the spongy road he stopped me.

'I know the very place.' he said, 'It goes up and down like a Portrush dance floor.'

He explained that the road makers had found it impossible to prepare a proper foundation. They had dumped tons of rubble to make a solid bed, but it was all swallowed up by the bog.

'There's no bottom to that bog.' He said it so solemnly, we knew we were meant to believe him.

Eventually the problem was solved by placing large logs across the line of the route and dumping rubble to weigh them down and so to build up the bed of the road. The tarmacadam surface was then laid on top.

Our friend had been serious for long enough and he looked at us both in turn, eyes twinkling, nodding his head to one side.

'So now we have in this district, the only road in Ulster which floats in the bog on a raft of logs.'

The way he said it made it sound a reasonable explanation, or was it? Was he still pulling our legs? Stanley and I looked at each other, wondering if we should believe him.

It was a fascinating evening, with interesting stories and the fun of the farmer's gentle bantering. They left before it became late, to give us the chance of an early night.

'You'll want to get to bed soon.' said the wife, 'After that long run to-day you'll need the rest. But you are your own bosses now and no doubt will please yourselves.'

As they left, the farmer turned back,

We're in for a heavy night's rain to-night.' he said kindly. 'Why don't you sleep in here? You could make yourselves comfortable in front of the fire.'

The looks on our faces must have been answer enough. It had to be the tent. We had come on the journey as campers and had to sleep out.

'Well.' he said 'If you're washed out of your wee tent you can always swim back across the farmyard to the comfort of the house here. Either way, we'll see you in the morning, no doubt ready for the road again.'

When they had gone, we pulled the easy chairs closer to the huge open fireplace and watched the embers glow and the blue flames leap.

We were tired and talked out and it was time for bed, but this was a comfortable place and neither of us wanted to move.

Without being aware of the reason, I find myself immediately at home in some places which are new to me and which I have happened upon in the course of a journey. It might be an ancient inn or a church or a castle. I might have become aware of the feeling as I found a camp or bivouac site high in the mountains. This affinity with some places manifests itself as a feeling of ease and tranquillity and a sense of familiarity, for which I have no explanation.

The room in the cottage is one of my earliest recollections of this feeling and, although it might appear to be readily explained by the security and comfort it offered, these advantages have been present, on occasions, in places which have seemed less than welcoming, even hostile.

On that evening, Stanley and I were completely at our ease in this room. Eventually we banked the fire with turf, as I knew we should and left the familiarity of the warm hearth for the dark and the orchard.

The tent looked a little more cheerful once we had lit the candle but it felt damp and cold after the cottage. We decided to keep our clothes on and I made a pillow with my shoes wrapped in my cycle cape. One blanket each seemed a miserably thin covering, but we had to admit, that carrying two or three each would not have been on.

I leaned across and blew out the candle. The rain started with a squall which flapped the side of the tent. Lying down again I tugged the blanket over my head and around my body so snugly that only my face was free. The rain was heavier now and I felt a fine spray on my cheek. Our little white tent was leaking without even having been touched.

After a day when so much had gone well, it was a great disappointment. Stanley asked me quietly if I could feel the spray and I grunted assent. I turned on my side and listened to the rain drumming on the canvas. The apple trees creaked and strained and apples fell with a soft thump on the grass beside us or hit the tent and slithered down its side.

Neither of us would have admitted to being home-sick or afraid at this moment but our voices must have betrayed it to each other. At Boys' Brigade camp there would have been a tent full of friends for company and half a dozen other big tents nearby.

Here we were on our own and outside our flimsy shelter there was the night-time world of the countryside, about which we knew almost nothing. Eerie sounds were separated by short periods of silence which seemed so odd and disquieting. I felt that, if we lay very still and quiet, nothing which might harm us would know we were there.

Our blankets were now damp but there was no question of leaving the tent for the cottage. We had set out on our journey to cycle and camp our way around the country. We had told our friends at home that we would be sleeping in the tent and had made much of it with our new friends, the farmer and his wife. The day's cycling had gone well and now we would have to make the best of the night in the tent.

Suddenly the wet spray stopped. It was still raining hard but the canvas was now keeping it out. At the time, we were not aware of the reason, but the yarn of canvas swells as it becomes wet. This reduces the size of the pores of the material, making it more waterproof when wet than when dry. However the fact that it had happened, gave us something cheerful to talk about and being able to praise the tent made us feel better. Soon we were too tired to stay awake any longer and went to sleep to the sound of the rain pattering on the canvas.

It was early and we were cold and stiff when we woke, but the rain had stopped. The farmer and his wife were already up and about and they waved to us as we made our way to the cottage to cook breakfast.

There was still a faint glow in the ashes on the hearth and I brought the fire to life as I had learned to do as an evacuee. Then I had been keen to go out to the big barn to fetch the driest, oldest pieces of turf and help Mrs Hodges, the farmer's wife with the fire. After breakfast, she always let me help with the milking, showing great patience and forbearing.

Here, in County Tyrone, I worked carefully and confidently, stacking small, crisp pieces of turf on the embers and fanning them with the lid of a pot. The fire glowed and flamed. Soon we were boiling the water for tea and frying bacon, eggs and bread in the big, iron pan.

As we sat down to the food, the farmer's wife looked in to see how we had survived the night. She was clearly impressed by the feast in front of us.

'There's one thing I'm sure of,' she said, smiling, 'While there's any food about, you two will never starve for want of somebody to cook it for you.'

We smiled in appreciation of the compliment and, when she had gone, I told Stanley that my father had no time for the commonly-held idea that cooking was an unmanly pursuit and the exclusive preserve of women and sissy men. He was fond of saying that any man worth his salt should be able to make a decent meal. He would have approved of our breakfast.

When we were packed and ready to leave, our new friends came out to see us off. They refused to let us pay for the potatoes, eggs and milk, insisting that they fill our milk bottle and that we take farls of fresh home-made soda bread to have at lunch time.

They looked sad to see us go. Stanley and I were both fair-haired and probably looked less than country-wise. This couple had taken on the anxiousness of parents and they were loathe to see us head off towards the unknown.

Years later, I came upon the advice of the Lebanese poet-philosopher, Kahlil Gibran in The Prophet, a book which he considered to be a part of himself. He could have been speaking to our parents or this fine couple.

'You are the bows from which your children as living arrows are sent forth.'

We mounted our loaded bicycles and prepared to leave.

'Keep pedalling.' said the farmer, 'You'll be in County Derry before you are properly started.'

'And don't forget Tyrone amongst the bushes.' said his wife, who looked close to tears.

We rode down the lane very slowly, wobbling as we turned to wave.

CHAPTER 8

Across Slieve Gallion's Foot

The main road went through Coagh but we could see on the map that it was possible to take a short-cut to Moneymore by turning off at Kingsmill. It was not sign-posted but it was a pleasant road and the route seemed to be straight-forward.

We crossed a river and the map showed that we were now in County Derry. Almost immediately we had our first clear view of the Sperrin Mountains. They looked dark, rugged, distant and seemed as if they might bar our way. There was no traffic, not even someone on foot to assure us we were heading for Moneymore.

The narrow road lay between the hedges and past occasional dwellings. Tyrone had been hillier than Armagh and now we had crossed into County Derry the hills seemed steeper and more frequent. Already the second day was proving to be much harder than the first.

It was a relief to ride down a long hill and to find Moneymore where we expected it to be. In the town people stopped work to have a better look at us. We rode slowly for, even though we were used to horse-drawn vehicles, it was a surprise to find so many in this part of the country.

In Belfast the Co-operative Society's deliveries of coal, milk and groceries were made from horse-drawn carts. The horses were usually huge, powerful animals, they needed to be for the loads were often enormous: the milk cart, in particular, carried as many crates as a small fleet of modern milk floats. The bread-cart was smaller and it was pulled by a lighter, quicker type of horse which trotted athletically into our street and, like the bigger horses, knew exactly where to stop.

Here, there were far more vehicles drawn by horse power. There were farm carts and brewer's drays, there were lighter carts with loads of vegetables, wood blocks, peat or builder's supplies.

In Moneymore we met a cheery man, with a pony and trap,

67

selling milk from big churns and, presumably, buttermilk too. A donkey, harnessed to a small cart loaded with manure, waited patiently outside a shop. We threaded our way through the traffic of the town, avoiding the piles of horse dung with a quick flick of the handle-bars, knowing not to cycle too close to the animals. I was fond of horses, my father had worked with them all his life and I knew he would be pleased to hear that there were so many of them here.

On the other side of the town there was a long, easy, straight stretch and then the road climbed steeply as if we were ascending into the heart of the mountains. We could see from the map that this was an out-rider ridge of the range and the real peak, Slieve Gallion, loomed above us on our left. It looked bigger and steeper than the Black Mountain and we were sure it must have been one of the hills we could see across Lough Neagh on the day we decided to make this journey.

We crossed Slieve Gallion's foot and the downhill spin on the other side was a help, but it seemed much shorter than the way up.

Desertmartin was friendly and decked with red, white and blue bunting and Union Jacks. In Tobermore a man waved to us. In spite of being tired the day was looking up. It takes so little to encourage someone who is making a physical effort, like a marathon runner or a long-distance cyclist, but a simple gesture of encouragement can have a most remarkable effect. We rode on to Maghera feeling that we were proper touring cyclists.

We were left in no doubt of the tribal allegiance of these small towns. The Orange Parades of the Twelfth of July celebrations were still over a week away but, in the appropriate places and probably some inappropriate places too, ceremonial arches had been built and the red, white and blue flags and bunting were flying. Huge mounds of burnable rubbish had been piled high for bonfires waiting for the Eleventh Night, the night before the main march.

In Belfast they were called bone-fires and I thought at the time, and in the ignorance of a little education, that this was our local mis-pronunciation. It was many years before I learned that, in past ages, bones had indeed been burned in such ceremonial fires. Our pronunciation of the word probably dated back to the English settlers at the time of the Plantations.

I wondered how many would march here in South Derry on the Twelfth. In Belfast the orangemen paraded by the thousand, with bands playing and banners unfurled, to a meeting place on the city's outskirts, called The Field. I had often seen them march and once, when I had been much younger, had been offered six-pence by a neighbour to join the walkers and carry a banner string. My father rarely interfered in anything I wanted to do, but on this occasion he was adamant. He did not approve of the marches and forbade me to have anything to do with them.

The Republican marching season was not until August but already, in some of these South Derry towns, the green, white and gold colours were appearing as if to mark out the territory and to show that the Republicans would not be outdone by the Orangemen.

We stopped in Maghera for a rest and checked our bicycles. We had never discussed their suitability for such a trip, but they were going well. They were so-called Sports Cycles, sturdily made, with three-speed gears and cable brakes. One of the boys in the Boys' Brigade had a machine of a different class, a proper racing bike. It was the real thing, with dropped handle-bars and an exceedingly complicated looking, but very efficient, five speed gear system which is still in production. The bicycle was so light it could be lifted on one finger, as he was fond of demonstrating. But then he was working and earning wages and we were still at school.

Although we were not complaining about our own machines, we talked about racing bikes and how they would take less effort to pedal uphill, or would be quicker on the flat, or far easier to push into the wind, crouching low over the dropped handle-bars.

On the previous day we had kept going with hardly a pause except to look at the map or eat, now we were finding it very difficult to cover the miles and realised that we had stopped in every town and village, using each one as an excuse for a break.

I had a mileometer attached to the front fork of my bicycle. Every time the front wheel revolved a small metal lug, firmly fixed to a spoke, touched and turned a cog on the side of the mileometer itself with a loud click. When we were bowling along at a decent speed the clicks tapped out a rhythm that kept me going well. It was the drum beat of the road.

On the previous day the tenths of miles had flashed by on the dial and the miles had steadily accumulated. However we had forgotten to note the starting mileage and, when we reached camp, had to measure out the distance we had travelled with a piece of string.

On this day the wheels turned slowly. The clicking beat of the mileometer was slow and dispirited. We made excuses for ourselves.

'We hadn't had a proper night's sleep. We'd come too far the previous day. The wind was against us. Our bicycles had only three gears. Our equipment was too heavy. It was all uphill.'

The truth was that we were not used to cycling any distance and on such a journey the second day is invariably harder than the first.

Maghera was a big place with wide, busy streets. It fitted exactly my idea of a market town and we stayed for a little while and watched its people at work.

On the other side, we climbed again and it was obvious that when we reached Swatragh we were back in the Sperrin Mountains. On this hilly terrain the cycling was proving very hard work. By the middle of the afternoon we decided that we had come far enough for the day and began to look for a place to camp. The mileometer showed that we had travelled thirty-five miles and, try as we might with our piece of string, we could make it no further on the map. It was much less than expected after the first day, but we were well on our way to the coast and refused to be disappointed.

I used the same tactic as the previous evening and asked a man by the road-side if he knew of someone who might let us pitch our tent. He was an elderly man who sounded abrupt, but his advice was helpful.

'Do you see that new house down the road?' he said. 'Ask them. They'll not turn you away.' He pointed to a farm some distance from the road.

The house looked newly built and we were met at the door by a young man who greeted us in friendly fashion as if he was glad to see us. This time I asked directly if we might pitch our tent for the night.

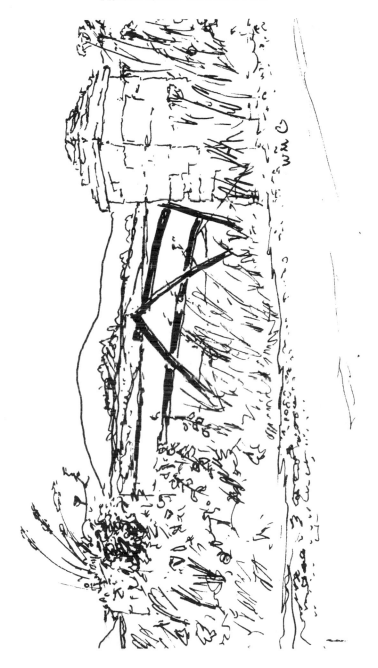

'No need to do that.' he said 'We've just moved into this new house and you can stay in the old one.'

As he spoke I was aware that there was a girl of his own age standing behind him. She laughed, squeezed past him and led the way across the yard.

'Sure the old house is still warm from last night's fire.' she said, 'We moved from there to here this morning.'

The old house, as they called it, was a cottage so like our haven on the previous evening it might have been the same place. It was a strange sensation, having stopped at random, to be offered the hospitality of a place so similar on the second day.

The young couple had left much of the old furniture behind and the cottage was warm and cosy, a ready-made resting place for two tired travellers. We could hardly believe our luck.

Would it be like this every night of our journey? Would there always be a comfortable cottage and friendly people to see us right?

During the day we had discussed the kindly welcome of the previous evening and come to the conclusion that it must be the special hospitality of County Tyrone, Tyrone amongst the bushes. But here we were in County Derry. The couple were younger and, although they had been surprised to see two boys of our age on a cycling trip, they too were welcoming us without hesitation or conditions.

We unpacked at the door as they watched and I found it hard to tell them about the previous night's camp, in case they thought we might be taking this kindness to travellers for granted. Once again, it was very difficult to explain that, although we were grateful to have the house to cook in, we wanted to camp.

They laughed at the idea of us sleeping out when we could be so comfortable inside, but eventually were persuaded and showed us an empty paddock where we could pitch the tent.

We never discovered whether they were brother and sister or man and wife but they treated us as if we were friends of the family. Without asking, the girl brought us eggs, milk, potatoes and home-made wheaten bread.

'Just a wee present to keep you going.' she said and slipped away as we were thanking her.

For the second time in two days we had landed on our feet.

We settled into the kitchen of the old house as easily as if we had been reared in the country. There was turf in a basket on the hearth and the open fire was easily lit. The crane over the fireplace swung out easily and we hung a pot of water from one of its chains. I pushed the crane back to let the water heat. It was always useful to have some hot water and it seemed a waste to have the fire burning and nothing heating on it.

There was a table and kitchen chairs, a sofa and a selection of pots and pans. On the deep window ledge sat a large paraffin lamp with a fancy glass shade, obviously in its accustomed place. It seemed as if this room had been specially prepared for us and was awaiting our arrival.

At first we thought it odd that the young pair had left so much behind them when they had made their move. We could see the new house through the window. It was a solid, two-storeyed, modern country house with a proper front door. But how could they have transferred the old furniture to their bright, new rooms and the pots from the open fire place to their brand new kitchen?

It was cold and overcast when we pitched our tent in the shelter of a hedge at one end of the paddock. Our blankets felt damp and we decided to bring them back to the cottage to be aired. The tent looked well on the outside but it no longer had our full confidence. Inside we spread out the groundsheet and it seemed so bare and uninviting as all our food and gear were across in the room.

Back in the cottage there was a pulley line at the back of the kitchen. We hung the blankets on the wooden bars and hauled it towards the ceiling. Once again it seemed that this place had been arranged specially to suit our needs.

In the early evening we washed potatoes and put them in a big pot on the fire to boil in their skins. We fried four eggs and opened our one tin of meat. When it was ready it looked like a feast. We ate the potatoes, skins and all. War-time food propaganda had taught us that the best part of the potato was immediately under the skin and that peeling before cooking meant that this good inner layer was lost to the refuse bucket. I also knew, from the book about travelling in the back-woods of America, that, although the skin of the potato was poisonous when raw, boiling removed the poison and the skins were safe to eat when so cooked.

As travellers, it seemed important to get it right and we discussed these matters seriously as we ate.

The fried eggs and potatoes with butter were so good together, the meat seemed like a luxury but we finished it as well, now that we had opened the tin. As yet our dried eggs were untouched because of the fresh eggs given to us by our hosts.

We agreed that on one of the evenings to come we would buy potatoes and have them with butter and scrambled eggs made from the dried egg powder. There was one small snag however, which we deliberately left unspoken. Here we had an open fire to cook on; without it we would only have the heat of one tiny spirit stove. It seemed best not to dwell on such difficulties when all was going so well.

If we had been depressed by our lack of energy during the day, the meal and this comfortable room cheered us wonderfully. It was also encouraging to see on the map, and by measuring carefully with the piece of string that we were about half way on our journey.

'Half way in two days.' We said it aloud. It sounded good. To-morrow we would reach the north coast and the prospect of camping near the sea was exciting. We cleared up and sat by the fire, stoking it with pieces of turf, like experts.

The top half of the door swung open and the girl's head appeared.

'Com'on over for a cup of tea.' she said. 'We're both dying to hear your chat.'

CHAPTER 9

Bacon and Egg Banjoes

Outside the back door there was a large mat and we wiped our feet with care, scraping the sides of our shoes along its edge for good measure. There were upright wooden chairs in the kitchen and we sat with our new friends in front of their new range.

Again it was a surprise to find our hosts so interested in us. They wanted to hear what it was like leaving Belfast for the wilds of the country; how we had been received in the towns and villages; what we thought of County Derry; where we had stayed the previous night; how far we had cycled in a day; why we had chosen their house.

It was the innocent curiosity of country folk, for whom the arrival of a stranger is a special event, a welcome break in the steady rhythm of life on the farm.

It is a scrutiny to which I have been subjected since, in remote homes in the rugged mountains of Iran and Afghanistan and at a lone house in a Himalayan valley, a full day on foot from the nearest village and three days from the nearest dirt road.

On my walk along the ancient pilgrim road to Santiago in Northern Spain a few years ago, I had met the same interested inquisitiveness. It was tempered there by acceptance, because so many pilgrims have passed along this way over the past one thousand years. It was only at the very end of that journey that it became a grand inquisition, when I sought, from the cleric responsible at the Cathedral of St. James, the scroll which would show that I had reached that mystical city on foot.

Here at this farm in County Derry, it was the gentle curiosity of new friends, anxious to share our adventure and we were at our ease.

The girl made a pot of strong tea and kept up a steady supply of home-made scones and buns. Once over our initial shyness, we found it so easy to talk to this young couple. We rambled on with our story, taking it in turns, keeping each other right.

We told them the tale of how hard the cycling had been that day, pushing uphill into the Sperrin Mountains, finding the hills far steeper and longer on the up side than on the down. They laughed at the very idea of these hills that were further up than they were down.

'No wonder you found it tough.' said the girl, 'Its only a few miles to the town and when I have to bike it, my legs aren't the better of it for days.'

Her husband or brother was encouraging.

'To-morrow it will be easier.' he said, 'You'll hit Coleraine and then the coast and you'll be on your holidays at the sea-side.'

That night it rained again and, when the fine spray wet our cheeks, we knew it would soon cease. The wind woke us, darting at the tent in sharp rushes, flapping the canvas, making it crack like a bull whip.

When the tent began to leak badly I blamed Stanley for letting the canvas touch his back. It was hardly his fault. The wind was gusting against his side of the tent and it would have been impossible for him to prevent the wet canvas flapping against him. With some reluctance, and probably bad grace, I moved over as far as I dared, to let him share my side.

Morning seemed a long time coming and it felt as if we had hardly had any sleep. But the day was bright and still, great weather for the road. We should have been tired after our troubled night but, once we were busy with breakfast, we seemed unaffected.

We fried the last of the bacon with the fresh eggs the couple had given us. I split two farls of soda bread and buttered them carefully while Stanley looked after the eggs. We put a whole fried egg and a rasher of bacon on one side of the split farl and placed the other side on top to make a sandwich. It seems a pity that affluence, or over-eating, or lack of exercise, or a combination of all three, have made most of us so wary now of the Ulster Fry. We made another sandwich and they looked so tempting they deserved a name. We called them our 'Bacon and Egg Banjoes'.

They took some skill in the eating, requiring speedy wrist work to keep the egg yolk in the sandwich rather than trickling down over our fingers and chins. They tasted so good we agreed we had never eaten anything so appetising.

Packing was a little easier, now every item had its own place in the kit and some rope, given to us by the girl, made the loads look much more secure.

They saw us off and were still waving as we turned the corner from their lane on to the road.

The breeze was against us, but we felt stronger than on the previous day. The cycling was easier. We were in good spirits and had made two more new friends.

As young travellers in a strange countryside, we had found friendship and country hospitality in this part of Ulster, which must have left its mark with us, beyond the journey and into our future lives. At our age and with our brief experience of life, we might have been forgiven for thinking that this was the way of the world, that wherever we went, it would always be thus. This good fortune occupied our conversation and thoughts and the miles passed quickly.

We left the hills of the Sperrins behind and cycled into Coleraine, crossing the River Bann in the middle of the town. The Lower Bann was a much more impressive river than the Lagan and we stopped on its bridge in admiration. It was wide, swirling, swift-flowing, surging impatiently towards the sea and the end of its journey. On the far side was a busy quay, with sea-going boats alongside. The water was a pale shade of brown, a much more natural colour for a river, than the darker waters of the Lagan.

A few years later I was to have more intimate contact with this formidable river, when I went with my school crew to row at the town's annual regatta. We struggled up stream in the rain to the start and, to try to raise our spirits, the cox kept telling us how helpful the flow of the water would be to us during the race.

Three eights took their places at the start and the rain was now much heavier. We were the Methodist College eight and to our right was the crew from the local school, Coleraine Academical Institution. On their right were the favourites, the crew from the Royal Belfast Academical Institution, our bitter rivals in all things sporting.

We started badly and immediately felt that we were rowing against both wind and tide. But it was the waves which created the

River Bann — Coleraine

most difficulty and they were being caused by the wind and the
tide running against the flow of the river. Racing boats are low to
the surface and each time we ploughed into a wave, we shipped
water.

   In a rowing eight the individual seats slide forward and backwards with each stroke. Everyone must keep in the same rhythm.
To take it easy, would mean a painful blow in the middle of the
back, as the oar of the crew member behind was pushed forward
to begin a stroke.

   We laboured from the beginning and lost sight of the other two
crews, as they forged ahead. Only the cox, who faces forward, can
see the opposition once a boat drops behind. He kept telling us
that they were just ahead, but we knew that was what he would
say, should they be a hundred yards in front. We plodded on, wet,
cold and increasingly despondent, but having of necessity, to
keep together, to continue to row as a crew.

   I was six from the front of the boat, but the spray still cascaded
over me each time we struck a wave. The race dragged on

interminably, without even a glimpse of our rivals. The bottom of the boat was awash. I struggled to keep rowing with my head down and, with each stroke, I could see the water swish back, then forward again around my feet. As I watched, a dirty bundle of sodden rags floated down between my legs and I realised that it was the bow man's brand new, and once exceedingly smart, white sweater, which he had stowed behind him at the start.

The cox screamed that we were catching the Belfast crew and that roused us for a final effort. As we passed them they began to sink. I had never seen a racing eight sink before. It did so in slow motion attended by a rescue launch. The boat had shipped so much water that it was full to the gunnels. It had given up the struggle within sight of the finish and was settling steadily and deliberately into the river.

A launch drew alongside, as the once elegant craft slipped below the surface and, ignominiously, the oarsmen were fished out of the water. We were a poor second to the Coleraine crew but it was good enough for us. We had beaten our real rivals and had the satisfaction of seeing them sink, as we stayed the course.

But that was all to come and, as Stanley and I watched this powerful river, we thought we were staying our course quite well. We admired the Bann, it was a proper river. In a way, it was a shock to find that Coleraine, which was not even a county town, had a much better river than the capital of the country. Coleraine was a likeable place, it was friendly, busy, bright and cheerful. I suppose, too, that it fitted perfectly, our optimistic mood of the day.

Beyond the town, we missed out Portstewart, which seemed to involve a detour, and reached the coast at Portrush. Although this was the time of post-war austerity, Portrush seemed to be a smart holiday resort. The hotels, shops and houses were perched on the little heights over-looking the harbour and the bay. To me, it looked a very grand place, shining in the sunshine, as if entitled to it, as of right. We free-wheeled along the main street and were impressed by the harbour and the relaxed atmosphere of the town. It was time for a stop but, on this day, we were in the mood for travelling and only paused for a few moments, before cycling on towards Bushmills.

Beyond the town, the road came back to the coast and we stopped again to identify The Skerries Islands on the map. A few miles further and there, in front of us, were the ruins of a most wonderful, fairy-tale castle. We dismounted and, for the first time in my life, I was in the presence of a real fortification, a stronghold of the ancient war-lords of Ulster.

We parked the bicycles to have a better look. The fortress was perched on a precipitous, rocky pinnacle, high above the sea, separated from the cliff of the mainland by a deep chasm. We guessed that once there had been a drawbridge, but were not to know that in its heyday, Dunluce Castle had five towers and grand apartments. Only two of the towers still stand, but enough of the battlements remained in this magnificent spot to excite our imaginations. In this location, it seemed impregnable, but it must have been attacked many times. We speculated about the ways in which the castle could have been assaulted, working out routes by which its cliffs might be climbed.

At the end of the 16th century the Mac Donnells salvaged heavy guns from the wreck of the Spanish Armada ship, the Gerona, and used them to defend this fortress. Later, the castle kitchen collapsed into the sea carrying nine servants to their deaths. Shortly afterwards, the Antrim family, who were in residence at the time, left Dunluce and moved their seat to Glenarm.

Had we known of it at the time, the dramatic past of Dunluce Castle would have been of the greatest interest to Stanley and me, but I doubt that it could have added to our sense of awe and wonder, when we made this spectacular discovery for ourselves. While we stayed, we talked a great deal about this formidable stronghold, placed in such a magnificent setting, but once on the road again, we were silent. Our imaginations needed time on their own.

The village of Portballintrae was small and picturesque, set above the sea but still a part of the shore. We considered stopping here but we were going well and decided to cycle a little further.

Bushmills was busy and businesslike. On the way out of it, we saw a sign for the Giant's Causeway and left the main road. A few miles further was the entrance to the Causeway Path and we discovered that, not only would we have to pay to get in, but that it was a fair walk to see the Causeway itself. Reluctantly, we decided that we could afford neither the money nor the effort and continued along the by-road.

Dunluce Castle

Portballintrae

It was a disappointment to have missed one of the Wonders of the World but it had seemed to be too much of a diversion from the journey. We told each other that there would be another time and, anyway, we had seen Dunluce Castle. And it seemed to be enough for one day.

Now that we regarded ourselves as experienced travellers, it seemed obvious that we would come back to this part of the north coast sometime soon. It was a relief too, to have saved the money. So far on the trip we had spent very little, having, of course, very little to spend. Our budget allowed a small sum for food each day and we had kept within that. There was no money for luxuries like overnights, or lemonade, or fish and chips, or entrance fees to Wonders of the World. Our mothers had given us a little extra 'for emergencies'. That was still intact, tied up in a corner of a hand-kerchief, and it was meant to remain so, unless it was really needed.

It was now near the end of the afternoon and we had come far enough. We cycled slowly onwards and met the main road as it reached the coast again. It would have been pleasant to camp on the shore, but the road was still high above the sea and we were looking for a farm as friendly as those we had found on the previous evenings.

I decided to try to use the tactic of the first day and, when we came upon a man fixing a fence by the road-side, it was too good a coincidence to ignore.

CHAPTER 10

No Room at The Manse

The man mending the fence examined us and our bicycles with care. His look said that this was someone used to appraising both humans and beasts. He seemed friendly and interested, glad to have an excuse to down tools and chat. He propped himself against the bank, high enough to look us in the eye as we leaned on our bicycles, waiting for us to speak first.

We started slowly, tentatively, and soon we were chatting to him as if we had known each other for years. The talk was about the weather, the state of the roads of North Antrim, Dunluce Castle and our decision to miss the Giant's Causeway.

'You did the right thing.' he said. 'You'll be back to this part of the world and the Causeway will still be here.'

He was most impressed that we had cycled so far in three days and delighted to hear that we were enthralled by the castle. Eventually, I raised the question of a place to camp.

'There's a youth hostel over there.' he said, pointing further up the road and in the direction of the sea.

To his amazement, neither Stanley nor I had ever heard of youth hostels. He told us that young people came to stay the night and that there was an office in Belfast.

'But if you haven't heard of the Association, you won't be members, so you won't be allowed to stay.' It was said gently but the logic of the situation left no room for further questions.

'Cheer Up.' he said 'You wouldn't want to stay there anyway. The man in charge is a miserable rascal. Nobody can agree with him. They call him the warden, but jailer would be a better name for him. He makes the visitors lives a misery while they're there.'

The fence-mender was not to know, but it was a relief not to be eligible to stay at the hostel and not because of the tyrant of a warden. There was sure to be a cost and money for overnights was not something we had included in our budget. Even more important was the fact that we intended to camp each night and, having refused comfortable sleeping quarters in the cottages on the previous two evenings, we could hardly seek a bed in a hostel, now we had come this far.

'Never mind.' said the man. 'The minister lives nearby and I know him well. He has just let most of his land, but the beasts are already grazing it and they would give you and your wee tent no peace.' He paused, raising his fore-finger towards us, to indicate that he had something very important to say.

'The point is.' he said, nodding his head wisely, 'The minister has kept a big paddock behind the house, to graze the child's pony and the pony doesn't arrive until next week.'

He smiled broadly, obviously delighted to be able to help us and waved us on our way towards the house.

'The minister won't turn you away.' he shouted after us. 'He'll let you use his outside tap for fresh water. Tell him I sent you.'

Stanley and I were elated. It had been a great day on the bikes and here we were, with every chance of yet another good place to camp.

The minister's house was at the end of a drive-way on the landward side of the road. The big paddock, the fence-mender had mentioned, was behind the house and we stopped beside it, leaning our bicycles against its fence. I walked across to the front of the house and knocked on the door.

It was opened by a man wearing a dark grey suit and a clerical collar. He frowned when he saw me and looked across at Stanley and the loaded bicycles.

'Well?' He said the word loudly as if I was standing some distance away.

It did not seem like the right time for casual conversation and the indirect approach, so I abandoned the usual tactic and asked him straight out.

'We're looking for a place to pitch our small tent for one night.' I said in a rush, 'We're cycling around Northern Ireland. This is our third day. We started from Belfast.' I was trying to sound friendly and confident.

He stared at me and glanced again towards Stanley and the bicycles.

'You've come to the wrong place.' He made it sound like a rebuke. 'I've no land for camping.'

My face must have been the very picture of amazement.

'But the man fixing the fence said … the big paddock at the back … the pony isn't coming until …' The surprise of his answer kept me talking as I searched for a way to say something that would not sound as if I was accusing him of telling lies.

The man interrupted, his unfriendliness turned to irritation.

'I've already told you I have no place for you to camp.' He said it so loudly that I was sure Stanley must have heard. 'The land is let, all of it is let.'

I stepped back and started to say 'Thank you.' but he had already turned away and the door swung shut with a dull, wooden clunk. Stanley was looking at me in disbelief as I walked towards him. It turned to despair when I relayed the whole conversation.

'Something must have happened to put him in a bad mood before I knocked the door.' I said apologetically. 'He says his land is all let.'

Somehow, it seemed to be my fault. Perhaps I should have tried the indirect approach and talked to the man first, before asking the question.

Stanley shook his head and began to re-tie the pack on the back of his bicycle, which he had begun to remove, in confident anticipation of the kind of welcome we had received before. For both of us, it was disillusionment on a grand scale and not only because we had failed to find a place to camp.

Our families were members of the Methodist church to which our Boys' Brigade Company was attached. There, the minister was respected by the congregation and deservedly so.

Although I was beginning to question evangelical teaching, I had the greatest admiration for our minister. It was by no means the first time I believed an adult was telling me a lie, but this should have been different. The minister might have been telling the truth and the man at the roadside misleading us. Or we might well have misunderstood. Whatever was the right way of it and because of our reception on the previous evenings, we found it hard to accept that a clergyman might treat strangers so inhospitably.

However, I refused to let it get me down. We still had to find a place to camp. Suddenly, I had an idea and my spirits rose on a wave of determination.

'If the man fixing the fence was wrong about the minister, he might be wrong too about the warden of the hostel.' I told Stanley. 'We'll ask the warden for a place for the tent.' It was probably said in a way which clearly meant that there was to be no argument.

We cycled along the driveway, without a backward glance at the manse and its paddock. The lane to the hostel was marked by a green triangular sign and we stopped at a whitewashed cottage to knock. Out of the doorway came a burly, red-haired man of middle height, thick-set, stern-faced and dressed in working clothes. He was younger than the minister and perhaps a few years older than the young couple we had stayed with on the previous night.

'I'm the warden.' he said gruffly. 'Where are your membership cards?'

'We're not members.' I said it as diplomatically as I could. 'We're looking for somewhere to camp. We didn't know there was such a thing as a youth hostel.'

The man leaned back against the door post and began to laugh, surprisingly gently at first for such a powerful looking man, then more loudly. He shook his head from side to side and held his sides as if it was the funniest thing he had heard in years. But it was obvious that he was not laughing at us.

'Good for you.' he said, when he had recovered himself. 'So you're on your own.' He chuckled, as he studied us and our bicycles with the eye of an expert.

'You've come a long way.' It sounded as if he understood what it was like to cycle a distance and he listened intently as we described our route around the country. We told him about our encounters with the fence-mender and the minister but, suspecting that they might have enough reasons already to be enemies, I gave no hint of the fence-mender's opinion of him.

He began to laugh quietly again.

'So there was no room at the manse.' he said 'I'll bet he didn't tell you to come to see me.' He winked and pulled his front door to.

'Follow me,' he said 'and I'll show you the best camp site in the

North. Even better than that, I'll show you the best free camp site in Ireland.'

We left our bicycles in a shed near his cottage and he led the way down a rough, narrow lane until we could see the shore.

Spread out before us was a large U-shaped bay with a sandy beach. It was hemmed in by white cliffs at either end and a steep bank behind.

'White Park Bay.' said the hostel warden with pride. 'This is it, the most beautiful strand in the country. They've even called the hostel after it.'

He pointed downwards to a patch of grass above the sand and there was no need for him to say more. It would should suit us perfectly. We stood together, taking in the whole sweep of the bay.

'It might not be the best place for a tent during the high tides of Spring and Autumn.' he said quietly, 'But you'll be safe enough at this time of the year.' We could see what he meant.

'I don't expect you'll be using soap, so you can wash in the sea.' The warden grinned. 'But you'll have to use my outside tap for your drinking water.'

He was so relaxed and friendly that it was hard to credit that this was the same man described to us by the fence-mender. After a few minutes silence, as if he was giving us time to appreciate where we were, he spoke again.

'When you come up to the cottage for water, I can sell you milk and potatoes if you need them. You'll be well placed down there on White Park Bay. Stay as long as you want.' There was real pride in his voice, as if we were his special guests.

We walked up the path with him to collect our gear and carried it back to the strand. The hostel was an oddly-shaped, two-storied building, on a patch of ground over-looking the beach. The door was open, but there was no one about. We crossed a stream below it and walked along the sand to the place the warden had indicated. I left my load down and climbed the grassy bank behind to have a look around. There were good sheltered camp sites at that level but, up here on the height, we would be away from the sea. The warden had shown us the best spot.

It was a small, flat terrace, a stretch of grass which met the sand of the beach and was only a foot or so above it. In a few minutes we had our tent pitched like experts and we sat down outside it in

White Park Bay

the sunshine. The strand was deserted, but the sound of the waves falling on the shore made this no place for loneliness.

Our camp site no longer exists, except in the memory. Over the years, the sea has taken the little terrace away and the sand of the beach now meets the high bank behind.

Then it was a magical place, where the sea and the land met. From the tent, we could hear and see the waves rolling in. There was no need to wear shoes. In two strides we could leave the grass and feel the sand between our toes. It felt as if we were camping that night in the very heart of the bay.

For a few moments, I was afraid to speak. It was such a transformation of the fortunes of the day, that talking about it might have changed the scene back to the driveway at the minister's house.

Here we were, with our very own strand. It was a much more wonderful and exciting prospect than either of us could have imagined.

It seemed obvious now, that the purpose of our journey had been to find this place and the farms we had stopped at in Tyrone and Derry. I had never been here before nor had I heard its name, but it seemed strangely familiar.

Had I always known about this haven in my secret dreams?.

CHAPTER 11

'Nae Breed Coupons! Nae Breed!'

We went back to fetch water from the tap at the warden's house and he sold us some milk. He looked pleased, when we told him about our great camp site.

'You don't need the hostel.' He said, nodding his head towards the building. 'You couldn't be better placed with your wee tent down beside the strand and not a soul to bother you.'

Neither of us had packed our bathing trunks and the water was cold when we took off our shoes and socks to paddle. The waves splashed up around our knees and sucked at our feet and ankles as they retreated. The coarse grains rasped across the skin and the sand pulled away from under our feet. We heard sounds from the direction of the hostel; an occasional shout and high-pitched laughter carried across the strand.

The hostellers must be enjoying themselves, we reckoned, but we saw no one. They were, apparently quite happily, confining themselves to their own premises. The bay remained our private demesne.

We discussed joining the Youth Hostel Association when we returned home, wondering what it would cost and how much we would have had to pay for an over-night. Within a year I had become a member and was pleasantly surprised to meet other young people who, like Stanley and me, wanted to travel the countryside.

The Association is still flourishing in Northern Ireland, although the method of travel is no longer usually on foot or by bicycle. Many of those who become members locally no longer visit hostels in Ireland. They join to use hostels abroad. However, even in these troubled times, a balance is achieved because well over half of the over-night users of hostels in Northern Ireland are from foreign countries.

This exchange of youth travel is an achievement of the very

greatest significance, but the youth hostel movement receives neither the public nor the official encouragement which it merits. Perhaps, as the new Europe emerges within the next few years, this contribution to international understanding, through the travelling of the young, will be accorded due recognition and support.

Stanley and I walked along the water's edge on our strand, wishing we could spend a few days here, exploring the cliffs and the village. We fancied ourselves as beachcombers, poking about in the washed-up debris, catching fish on a long line, collecting drift wood for a fire to cook the fish, learning about which shell fish we could eat, searching at the tide line for a bottle with a message in it.

Hunger made us think about cooking the evening meal and, for the first time, we were faced with using the tiny stove. I filled it from the bottle of methylated spirit, carefully pouring the fluid through the mesh at the top. It lit easily and burned with a blue, wavering flame. We tested its efficiency with a little water in one of the pots. The time passed and the water became lukewarm but seemed reluctant to come to the boil. Obviously, this little stove would not produce enough heat to cook the few potatoes we had left, nor would we be able to make tea.

We set out the remaining food on the ground sheet. As well as the potatoes we had the milk we had bought from the warden, some butter, tea and a little jam. Our benefactors on the previous evenings had given us home-made bread, which we had used first and we had a few slices of the white loaf left which we had brought from home. To some it might have seemed stale, but to us it looked good.

There was one more item which we had carried the whole way from Belfast, as yet untouched. It was the grey, waxed carton of American dried eggs. It had caused a little amusement at the farms and our friends there had insisted that we take some proper eggs and keep this lot for an emergency. The one dish, which I knew needed only the gentlest of heat, was scrambled egg. Now was the time to try it.

We discussed the number of reconstituted eggs we thought we could eat, and decided to make up enough of the dried powder to produce a dozen eggs. The mixture could be cooked in melted butter and served on slices of buttered bread. It sounded good, and even better than that, it seemed possible.

During the war years, dried egg had sometimes been a topic for complaint and often the subject of humour. Fried, it was reckoned to be best suited for soling shoes and cooked in any way, was supposed to have added a new depth of meaning to the old saying that 'eggs are binding'.

The few who truly appreciated dried eggs knew, however, that the secret lay in its reconstitution. It was essential to measure out the quantities of dry powder and water with some accuracy. It was also necessary to add the water cold and a little at a time, to make a smooth, even paste without lumps. This much I knew and had practised before leaving home.

I made the paste in one pot with great care and poured the mixture on the melted butter in the second pot. There seemed to be a great deal of the liquid egg. The pot was almost full and, as the stove was not stable enough to leave the pot sitting on top, I had to hold it in place.

Stanley watched hopefully, making encouraging noises. The flame wavered and flickered and seemed no more powerful than a single candle. We moved the stove into the doorway of the tent to give it as much shelter as possible.

It was necessary to change hands, to rest the arm holding the pot, but there was no sign of the liquid starting to cook. I was expecting it to sizzle and plop like proper scrambled egg but the mixture was as still and inactive as cold, thin porridge. Doubt and disappointment began to take over from the excited anticipation of another good meal.

I gave the mixture a stir, just to show Stanley that I was trying and felt a slight thickening at the bottom. He was allowed to check and he agreed. A few minutes later, there was a plop on the surface and we knew that the cooking had properly begun. Never was a pot so conscientiously watched. I stirred gently, aware that cooking eggs stick to the bottom and burn. I need not have been concerned. Our flame was so gentle, it was cooking by warming rather than by heating.

Stanley had the bread buttered and waiting, but the eggs were in no hurry and we had to be patient. They began to fluff upwards and look appetising. The smell was like the real thing. I dropped another lump of butter into the middle and we agreed that it was ready to serve. As fairness demanded, the portions looked exactly similar and we took our laden plates and a mug of milk each, to the edge of the sand for the feast.

There could be no doubt about it. This scrambled egg was the best we had ever tasted.

We thought about trying to make tea and decided that the little stove had done its work well enough for one day. Instead, we had some more milk and a slice of bread and jam each. It had been a much simpler meal than those we had been able to cook on the open fires on the previous evenings. But now that we had used our own stove, we felt like real campers.

Cleaning the pot was easier than expected. Stanley stood ankle deep in the sea and scoured it clean with a handful of sand. We cleared up and tidied around the tent. The blankets and kit were not arranged in the precise, military fashion required for a BB inspection, but every item was neatly stowed in its place and we were pleased with our efforts. To us the camp looked as if it had been pitched and looked after by experts.

Later, we walked again along the high tide mark in our bare feet. At one end of the bay, below the cliffs, was the tiny village of Portbraddan. The name means 'the salmon harbour' and its church is reputed to be the smallest in Ireland. We had noticed the name on the map earlier and had thought about walking across to it after we had eaten. There was no question of that now. We were happy where we were and the little hamlet-port seemed further away, cut off from us and our camp.

The waves rose, as they ran in towards the beach, slowly tumbling over as the crest formed and fell. It gave the illusion that the sea was higher than the sand of the shore on which we were standing. Try as we might, neither of us could explain this phenomenon. It was a bigger mystery than the tales we had heard of the stream which flowed uphill or the mountain road on which a car could free-wheel up the slope.

Our strand was still deserted and it felt as if all the nearby land was uninhabited and that we were entirely on our own. There was no unhappy feeling of being isolated. Rather, it was a reassuring sense of being in the right place.

A year later it returned, on a winter walk through the snow-covered Mountains of Mourne and, ten years after, I was aware of the same feeling on a small island off the west coast of Ireland, on which no one had lived for centuries. Here, on Whitepark Bay, it was as if we had somehow separated ourselves from the rest of the world.

Next morning we were up early and in great excitement. This might well be the last stage of our journey. If we did as well as the first day, we might reach Belfast by the evening.

The bread and milk were finished at breakfast and we agreed to buy more in Ballycastle. Stanley checked in his saddlebag for the bread coupons and I knew by the look on his face that he had not been able to find them. Bread had been rationed only recently and, in that period of immediate post-war austerity, its rationing was a serious business.

I knew I was being unfair, but that did not stop me blaming Stanley. Now that we had lost the coupons, bread suddenly became the most important item of food, the only thing that could be relied on to keep us going to the end of the journey.

We struck camp and carried our gear up the lane to the bicycle shed, without a glance back at White Park Bay. The bicycles were loaded in silence, Stanley feeling despondent, knowing what I was thinking. We thanked the warden of the hostel and cycled towards Ballycastle, still in irritable silence.

It was not far but the road was hilly. After Ballintoy we had to stand up on the pedals, in low gear, on the steepest climb yet. The effort took our minds off our problem and reaching the crest was a relief. Free-wheeling down the long slope between the woods and the sea to Ballycastle harbour was such a delight, we almost forgot to be grumpy with each other.

In the town the sun was shining and the people were bright and cheerful. Ballycastle seemed to be the most attractive place we had visited so far but my worst predictions were fulfilled when we found a shop.

It had been a shock to have such a basic food as bread rationed, now that the war was over and most shopkeepers were keeping strictly to the regulations. Had we been known locally, it might have been different. Perhaps we went to the wrong shops. But none of the shops we tried would sell us a loaf without the coupons. It seems hard to credit now when I visit Ballycastle, one of the friendliest and most hospitable places in the whole country, but on that day we were not able to buy bread.

We decided that there was nothing for it now but to head for home. We toiled up the steep hill out of Ballycastle feeling tired, lonely, dispirited and sorry for ourselves.

When we reached the open mountain, there was a little sense of achievement or perhaps it was relief. This had to be the top of the last of the big hills we had to climb. Our spirits rose and we cruised across the hills, going easily, suddenly feeling stronger than we had done since the first day.

Now we were friends again, laughing about the loss of the coupons and imitating the voices of the good shopkeepers of Ballycastle, as they refused us our daily bread.

'No bread coupons! No bread!' we yelled at each other and then, trying the North Antrim accent.

'Nae breed coupons! Nae breed!'

It did the shopkeepers of that lovely sea-side town less than justice but making a little fun of them cheered us up.

On high ground above Cushendun, crossed by the road from Ballycastle, is the famous Vanishing Lake of Loughareema, or Loughaveema, as it is named on some maps. Sometimes after heavy rain, the lake floods and the water flows across the road. In dry weather it can vanish, as its water seeps away through fissures in the chalk. With great seriousness, we discussed its disappearance without obvious cause and its subsequent reappearance in equally mysterious fashion. Unlike the illusion of the sea appearing higher than the shore, this time we both knew the secret.

However, learning about the Vanishing Lake in a Geography lesson in the class-room, like hearing of other dramatic physical features, had seemed no more real than Cowboys killing Indians on the cinema screen. Now we had reached the lake and could see for ourselves. It was full to overflowing and its water threatened to flood the road. We were suitably impressed.

The view from the top of the Black Mountain, of the land of Ulster spread out around us, had had the same effect. Geography was not just another school subject, like Algebra, which had to be

Cushendun

studied to pass examinations. We knew that it was about the shape and nature of the world.

Freewheeling down Glendun, we reckoned that cycling must be the way to travel. Glendun means 'the brown glen', but it was green, bright emerald green in the sunshine.

We missed out Cushendun and, on the way to Cushendall, two mountains stood out above the plateau. We checked the map and only one was named. On the right was Trostan and ahead, the unnamed peak could only have been Lurigethan. It was not high enough to be marked on our map but, as we descended towards the sea, it rose above us. Viewed from here it is perhaps the most beautiful peak in the Hills of Antrim.

Soon we were beyond Cushendall, touring along with the wind behind us, following the coast road between the cliffs and the sea.

Waterfoot seemed to me to be a most interesting name for a village, set as it was across the mouth of the valley and between steep hills on either side. The road was good and we were going well, closer friends now that we had managed to cope with the difficulties of finding a place to camp the previous evening and the loss of the bread coupons.

It was a spectacular place to be, below the white chalk and dark basalt cliffs. It felt like the first day again, speeding along with the mileometer clicking away to a beat that kept me pedalling in its rhythm. We chatted and joked about how quickly we would make it back to the city. The Antrim Coast Road must be one of the finest scenic roads in Europe and at the time we were impressed. To us, it seemed a dramatic feat of engineering to have carved a ledge for this road at the foot of the cliffs.

But all was going too well again and, if the misfortunes of the beginning of the day were behind us, we were not yet safely home.

My rear tyre burst with a bang that stopped us in our tracks, me as the wheel rim hit the ground and Stanley because of the noise. Without me being aware of it, my tyre had split and the inner tube had pushed its way through the hole to form the kind of bubble that we called a bunion. As the bunion got bigger, it rubbed on the forks and exploded. It left me with a badly holed inner tube and a three inch split in the tyre.

In the repair kit I had a strip of rubber which we used to line the tyre and that seemed as if it might hold. The inner tube was much

Lurigethan

Cushendall

more difficult to fix because of the size and shape of the hole. We mended it as best we could, pumped up the tyre as gently as possible and tried it out. It seemed fine but after a mile or so I had to get off and reinflate.

I tried to buy a tyre in the next village but there was none for sale. Bicycle spares were very hard to come by in these times of austerity and the man at the garage advised me to make the best of it until I reached home.

As the miles slowly passed, the distance between the stops for pumping up the tyre shortened. Although it was a most exasperating process, we managed to keep our spirits up by trying to joke about our predicament. Later it was easier to share the funny side of it with our friends ... me pumping up the tyre, jumping into the saddle and pedalling furiously to gain a few hundred yards before the tyre became flat again.

By mid-afternoon and, in spite of this erratic method of progression, we had covered over fifty miles from our camp. Now the distance between each reinflation was down to twenty-five yards. By the time we reached the outskirts of Larne, the tyre no longer responded to my best efforts to pump it up and we decided that the cycling part of my journey was over.

Waterfoot

Waterfoot

CHAPTER 12

The Secret of The Traveller's Holy Grail

I walked into Larne and Stanley rode beside me, at my pace. Slow cycling is an art form but we had practised it often enough for slow bicycle races in the street at home. It involves much wobbling of the handle-bars, moving the front wheel rapidly to and fro, to keep balance. Although it was much more difficult with the load of camping gear on the back, Stanley was able to cope and, if he happened to gain a few yards, he circled back and came up beside me again. He chatted cheerily as he rode and I walked, stiffly at first, feeling saddle-sore, then more easily as I found the right pace.

I was concerned that the weight of the gear over the back wheel would damage the rim as it revolved on the flat tyre. A buckled rim was much more serious than a burst tyre, so I kept one hand under the saddle and tried to lift the weight off the wheel on the rough parts of the road.

The road into Larne was pleasant, with grand houses and a view across the sea to the Maidens Rocks. The peninsula of Island Magee looked very close across the mouth of Larne Lough and it was easy to see how it ensures that the port has a sheltered harbour.

The railway station, when we found it, was quiet and empty, as if its work was over for the day. We used the money we had with us for emergencies to buy the tickets and sat on a bench to wait for the train. If Stanley was disappointed at the way we were finishing our journey, he made no mention of it. The last of the chocolate was a treat and we talked about our adventures, finding it very easy to agree about our impressions. Reckoning up the distance covered so far took careful checking on the map and calculating from the mileometer. It worked out to be about 170 miles to Larne Station. There was nothing we knew of, which would help us

Cave Hill

judge this as an achievement. But it felt as if we had come a long way.

We travelled back to Belfast in style, with the bikes in the luggage van and ourselves stretched out in comfort, with a third class carriage all to ourselves. The railway line hugged the coast-line, first along Larne Lough, then by the open sea and Belfast Lough. It was a strange feeling to be travelling without having to make a physical effort to do so. This, we reckoned, was luxury.

It was probably a slow train, stopping at every halt. To us, used as we were to seeing the countryside at cycling pace, the train fairly sped along. On one side the landscape rushed by, and on the other side, the seascape was further away and passed our window not nearly so quickly.

Cave Hill stood high on the sky-line and we knew we were approaching the city. The first signs of the outskirts of Belfast appeared and the train began the long process of slowing into York Road Station.

The bikes had travelled as comfortably in the guard's van as we had in our carriage and the ticket collector stood back to let us through. The station is on the north side of the city and it was still five miles from home. Again Stanley demonstrated his skill at slow cycling and I walked, pushing my bike.

Most of the city thoroughfares were surfaced with square-setts and the back wheel bumped over them on its flat tyre. I did my best to save the rim, by trying to raise the saddle a little but it was a strain on the arm and I had to keep changing sides. The walk seemed longer, through the streets of the city, than I thought it would be, but it was increasingly familiar ground. We took a short cut from Great Victoria Street to Sandy Row. The pavement was crowded and the shops were full of people. It was very much busier than anywhere else we had been on our trip, as if every day here was a market day.

On the Donegall Road there was a short, steep hill outside the Public Library and a sign said ...

CARTERS. GET DOWN OFF THE CART
AND LEAD THE HORSE UP THE HILL.

I reckoned I knew how the horse felt as I pushed my bike and its load up the slope. Around another bend we saw The Monarch Laundry. We were almost there.

On that last stretch of our journey, tiredness was of no account. We parted company at the corner of his street without saying much but we were closer friends now than we had been when we started.

When I reached home, I went around to the entry at the back and let myself into the yard. My mother was surprised that the trip had not taken a few days longer but she was relieved, as well as pleased to see me.

Her first concern was not how far we had cycled or even where we had been. She wanted to know where we had stayed at night and how we had managed for food. Being from the country herself, she was delighted that we had been so well received at the farms in Tyrone and Derry.

I decided not to tell her about our disappointment with the minister in North Antrim. It would have annoyed her more than it had us at the time. Instead, I mentioned the helpfulness of the hostel warden and she agreed that it would be a good idea for me to join the Youth Hostel Association with future trips in mind.

She relaxed when I told her about the cottages and cooking on the open fire.

'And I thought this connection had left all that behind us when I left Magheralin to come to live in the city.' she laughed, again I think, with relief.

The story of cooking the scrambled egg on the methylated spirit stove intrigued her.

'I wondered how you would manage on that wee stove.' she said, after a pause, 'But you surely picked the right dish to cook on it.'

She was not one to be lavish with compliments and that was praise indeed.

'By the way,' she continued, 'I must show you how to scumble eggs. You will like them even better than scrambled.'

It was her way of showing her approval. In our family, I was never short of encouragement but praise was rarely spoken. It was communicated very effectively in other ways, by looks, by the attitude to me, by practical support, by knowing that, no matter what, they were on my side.

When my father came home, his face told how he felt. I could see he was delighted that the trip had gone so well and his look to my mother said quite plainly,

'I told you it would be all right.'

That evening, Stanley and I met our friends who had been on the Black Mountain with us. They interrogated us on every detail of the trip, questioning every reply, asking for confirmation from one of us when the other answered. At least it showed that they were interested. Had they not been, a studied lack of concern would have defeated any effort we might have made to entertain them with our adventures.

The full story took several days to tell, for although they wanted to hear it and we were keen to re-live our experiences, their attention was easily diverted to some more immediate happening.

We made them laugh as we acted out the incident of the puncture, me jumping off an imaginary bicycle to pump up the tyre, then leaping back on to pedal furiously as far as I could before the wheel bumped on the ground again. Stanley demonstrated his expertise as a slow bicycle rider.

One of our friends asked if any of the people who had befriended us were Catholics. It was an innocent question, asked merely out of interest. But once it was put to us, the answer seemed important, much more so than the questioner meant it to be.

We told them that, with one exception, we had no idea of the religion of the people we had met. They looked puzzled, wondering if we were trying to hide something from them. Surely, they reasoned, it must have been obvious which side of the house these people were.

What about holy pictures on the wall? What about their names? What about the way they talked? Did they say 'hatch' or 'etch'? Did they not have their flags out for the Twelfth?

In our part of Belfast it was possible to reach adulthood without getting to know even one Catholic. We lived in different areas. We went to separate schools. Each Church provided for the social life of its own congregation. All the youth clubs and all the uniformed youth organisations were church based. Our Boys' Brigade Company kept us interested and occupied with sessions every week-day evening. There was football and swimming on Saturdays and Bible Class on a Sunday afternoon. When I went to train as a teacher, I found that there were separate colleges for Catholics and Protestants. It had the required effect and kept each of us to his or her own.

However, shortly after our return from the journey I realised that there was something seriously amiss. A man whom I greatly admired, a committed Christian who had dedicated his life to the service of others, was taking the morning service one Sunday as a lay preacher. During the course of his sermon, as he challenged the doctrine of the Roman Catholic Church, he raised his voice and found himself carried away in a bitter attack on Roman Catholics in general. The anger lasted only for a few moments and then he stopped in mid-sentence, as if suddenly aware that he had shocked both the congregation and himself.

His Methodist audience might have accepted that the Roman Catholic Church was fair game but attacking people who happened to be Catholics would have been perceived as un-Christian and not fitting for a preacher in their church. He might have been speaking aloud their secret fears but they expected to hear from the pulpit the gospel of 'love thy neighbour'.

The preacher left his harangue suspended where he had stopped and, after a decent pause, continued in a lower tone on the much sounder basis of the need to be saved from sin.

However, the effect on me of his lapse was immediate and profound. There was no question that I might lose my admiration for the man. He had earned that and was entitled to it. But for the first time I was truly aware of how great was the animosity of many Protestants for Catholics and how deeply they distrusted the Roman Catholic Church. It should not have been a shock. After all, I had lived here all my life. But it was such a contrast to the attitudes of my home up-bringing that it took this dramatic incident to reveal the true situation to me.

From then on I found it hard to accept the claim, which seems to be so fundamental to the doctrine of most churches, to have a monopoly of religious truth and to have exclusive rights to the services of God.

As Stanley and I stood on the street corner talking with our friends about the journey, it was obvious that they were not going to continue with their other questions until this important matter was cleared up.

'You might have been staying with Catholics without knowing it.' one of them said. It may have been a mild criticism but there was a pause and the questioner looked foolish, as the rest of us stared at him without speaking. We all began to laugh and he joined in as loudly as any of us.

'So what, if they dug with the other foot.' he said eventually. 'They certainly looked after you two all right.'

We found it hard to tell them why we had enjoyed ourselves so much; why we felt so close to the people who had befriended us; why we seemed to know our own country better now. But they understood. We all knew that it was not the achievement of covering the distance or overcoming the difficulties.

It was the prize for having been on such a journey.

It is even more important to know where to begin travelling than where to end. My pilgrimage began on the Black Mountain above Belfast.

Having reached that peak and seen the horizon march backwards, to show places I had only heard of before, it was obvious that the next route should be around my own small country.

The end of each stage reveals the beginning of the next.

Since those days, I have searched for the holy grail of the traveller in the Alps, the Pyrenees and the Arctic, in the mountains of Turkey, Iran and Afghanistan, and amongst the high peaks of the Himalayas themselves. I have walked on my own along the ancient pilgrim road to Santiago de Compostella in Northern Spain and south from there across the rivers of Portugal. On the third stage of that journey around the Iberian Peninsula, I have continued east across the Mountains of Andalucia in Southern Spain.

The real intent of the travelling has rarely been its declared purpose. But the further I go the more I feel in touch with the quest.

The secret of the grail is not to be found at journey's end but is the reward of being a hopeful traveller.

INFORMATION SECTION

Northern Ireland Tourist Board.
Publications include 'Where To Stay' price £2:50 (in 1990) and
'Stop And Visit' free.
Tourist Information Centre, High Street, Belfast. BT1
T/N (0232) 246609

Tourist Information is also available from each District, Borough
and City Council in Northern Ireland.
see the NI Telephone Book for telephone numbers.

Youth Hostel Association of NI
56 Bradbury Place, Belfast BT7. T/N (0232) 324733

Sports Council for NI. For cycling and walking information.
House of Sport, Upper Malone Road, Belfast. BT9 5LA
T/N (0232) 381222

The National Trust. For information on Trust Properties and the
North Coast.
Regional Office, Rowallane House, Saintfield, Co. Down.
T/N (0238) 510721

The Ulster Museum, Botanic Gardens, Belfast. T/N (02320 381251

The Ulster Folk and Transport Museum
Bangor Road, Holywood, Co. Down. T/N (0232) 428428

There are also excellent local museums throughout the Province.
For details contact the NI Tourist Board (see above) particularly
the 'Stop and Visit' booklet.
Information also available locally from the District, Borough or
City Council.

The Society for the Preservation of the Countryside. Welcomes
new members.
The Secretary, West Winds, Carney Hill, Holywood, Co. Down

ALSO BY THE SAME AUTHOR

PILGRIMS' FOOTSTEPS
by Bert Slader

For many years Bert Slader has had a special interest in the mountains of the Pyrenees. There he follows the old ways used by soldiers, travellers, and traders crossing between France and Spain and climbs the peaks by the routes used by the pioneer mountaineers of the last century.

On one solo journey across the range he came upon a much worn track near a high pass. It proved to have been a Roman road and used a thousand years later by the pilgrims of the Middle Ages on the way to Santiago de Compostela in the north-west of Spain.

In 1985 he set out on his own from France to walk the 550 miles to Santiago along the ancient pilgrim road.

PILGRIMS' FOOTSTEPS is his first book and is based on the experiences of that journey. He recounts the stories of the places and people he met along the way. He describes the inner journey of his thoughts and the effect on his beliefs and attitudes.

There is an Appendix on the country cooking of Northern Spain which includes recipes for regional dishes and an Information Section for those who wish to make the journey on foot or by car.

Illustrated by photographs and sketches by the author.

─ ─

PILGRIMS' FOOTSTEPS is available from:-

QUEST BOOKS
2 Slievenabrock Avenue, Newcastle, Co. Down, N.Ireland. BT33 0HZ.
Telephone (03967) 23359

© £5:75 per copy including U.K postage

For orders from the Rep. of Ireland:-
Please send the current IR£ equivalent of the sterling price + 50 pence to cover additional postage costs.

If you wish to have a signed copy please indicate this with your order and print the name or names to whom the copy should be dedicated.